THE
HIDDEN
H A L F
HIDDEN

Discovering the World of Unreached Peoples

Sam Wilson
Gordon Aeschliman

Scripture taken from the HOLY BIBLE: New International Version. Copyright © 1973, 1978 by the International Bible Society. Used by permission of Zondervan Bible Publishers.

Excerpts by Marilyn Laszlo taken from *Confessing Christ as Lord: The Urbana 1981 Compendium* edited by John W. Alexander. © 1982 by Inter-Varsity Christian Fellowship of the USA and used by permission of InterVarsity Press, Downers Grove, IL 60515.

Library of Congress Card Number: 84-062169
ISBN 0-912552-43-3

Content © by MARC, a ministry of World Vision, International

Published by MARC, World Vision, International, 919 W. Huntingdon Drive, Monrovia, CA 91016, U.S. of A.

This book is the result of many hours of loving help from the MARC and WORLD CHRISTIAN staffs. Without their help the two of us would not have been able to complete it.

Thanks for your patience, persistence and good humor.

Sam and Gordon

Contents

CHAPTER ONE

Peru, Passion and Prostitutes

Christians generally stay out of night clubs. But one night, a friend and I sensed very specifically that God wanted us to go into one. And there we met Michelle.

We were in Ensenada, 70 miles down the coast of Baja California, a city like hundreds of other third world cities. People on the move everywhere. Music blaring from a hundred speakers, all aimed at the street. Streets torn apart by potholes, choked with traffic, confused by erratic stoplights. Brightly painted buses fighting for road space with dented up taxis.

Homes too fragile to offer sufficient shelter from winter rains ring the city. Children playing listlessly in muddy yards show the sad signs of malnutrition and bad sanitation.

These needs had brought me to Ensenada scores of times. I used to lie awake at night thinking of the thousands who die senselessly each day. But hope grew in me as I saw hundreds of my college peers rise to the challenge of serving the people of Ensenada. "The hungry world isn't really hidden from us," I remember thinking. "All we need is help to know how to respond."

My first encounter with Michelle shook me up.

Her world was a part of Ensenada I had never seen before—one I would never have planned to enter. As

Jeff and I worked our way into the smoke-filled, raucous night club, the noise and sleaze engulfed us. The room roared with the wild yelling and laughter of men giving vent to their lust. The cheap, tinny, out-of-tune band seemed to mock the trapped women being offered as merchandise.

Michelle sat down at our table and recited her few English words to get a trick. We told her we only wanted to be friends. Several hours later, frustrated and overwhelmed by the utter lostness and degradation of the place, Jeff and I stood by our campsite. We just stood there in absolute silence for 45 minutes, thinking about the pain and abuse that filled Michelle's life.

Michelle's world stretched only the distance between her apartment and the club. The pimp viciously guarded her against intruders, and we soon realized why we had been prompted into the club—there was no other way into her life.

Her pimp used drugs to control her. Once, while dangling the drugs she desperately needed in front of her, he had made her sign a "performance" contract. She thought the only way out was prison.

Or suicide. Her wrists showed the attempts, but somehow she had never succeeded. Now God had guided us into her life. We spent much of the next ten days with her. And we began to see the hope of God restoring his beauty in her.

At one point, Michelle had turned to the church, looking for a way out of the traps of prostitution. But the pastor of the largest church in town told her to leave, because her presence would "defile the sanctuary."

Trapped and despairing, she bounced back and forth between drugs and hard liquor—up one minute and down the next. Performing.

The doors began to open for Michelle when Jeff and I managed to get her to the beach and spent the day reading story after story of Jesus' encounters with needy people. She felt his love in the account of the adulteress caught in sin: "Neither do I condemn you. Go and sin no more!" She gave her heart to him.

Michelle's life became my teacher. I saw how God loves all people and searches for the ones trapped in a world that bars them from knowing Jesus. I saw his love break through the darkness that held Michelle.

Hidden in Mongolia

Another friend told me of an encounter he had with people trapped by religious and political barriers, rather than the exploitation of Michelle's underworld. But the results were the same—people had no access to the love of Jesus until someone made the effort to enter their world.

"It must be the gate to hell"—that's how he described the Buddhist temple he visited in Mongolia.

He watched 40 monks engaged in their worship ceremony. They were lined up back to back in pairs and held bowls of rice and incense sticks. They beat drums in an uneven rhythm and chanted monotonously. Periodically they would throw handfuls of rice into the air. All at once, demon voices and growls came out of their mouths as they sat in trance-like postures.

"I've never experienced something as utterly evil and demonic," my friend said. "I just had to get out of there."

To most of us, Mongolia is a mystery. Hidden somewhere beyond the Bamboo or Iron curtains, its people, history and customs are as foggy as its location. But if Mongolia seems hidden from us, Jesus is all the more hidden from its people.

The government (a satellite of the Soviet Union) enforces the official policy of atheism. No missionaries are allowed in the country and no witnessing is permitted.

Trapped within this closed political boundary are over one million religious people (two-thirds of Mongolia's population) who are trapped a second time—in the clutches of Buddhism. Buddhism has dominated their world since the 1500's. Its institutions and practices have even survived the savage murdering of most of the priests by the government during the 1920's.

My friend described to me a conversation he had with a Mongolian man who had never heard of Jesus.

I asked Sukhe if Mongolian people ever wonder if God exists. He said yes. I told him that we believe Jesus Christ is God. I described God's character, telling how Jesus Christ is a good and loving God. He said, "Oh, it sounds too wonderful!"—as if he was not quite sure it could be real.

I told him about the Bible, and asked if he would read a Bible if he had one. When he said yes, I said, "I have a Bible written in Mongolian you can have."

He was astonished. "What did you say?" I offered it again and asked if he would read it.

He said, "Yes!" and I gave it to him. He seemed very pleased to receive it.

The next day, Sukhe was there waiting for us again. I asked if he had read the Bible. He said, "Yes, one-third of it."

"Did you understand it?"

"Yes, I did."

I asked what he thought about it. He searched for words, then said, "It was right."

"The truth?" we asked.

"The truth, yes." he said.

I asked if he had prayed. "I forgot what to say. Could you please write it down for me?" Then he asked, "Will I hear him?"

I explained that God has spoken audibly to people, but usually we hear him in a still, small inner voice.

He said, "Oh! I thought I would hear a loud voice." He wanted to know if we could see Jesus. I said no, because he has ascended into heaven.

"I wish I could see him now!"

Toward the end of our walk in the park some friends warned him that he was being watched. I noticed an officer checking someone's passport, so I said I had to leave.

He told me, "These have been the most wonderful days of my life. But it is difficult to talk."

Sukhe lives in the world of hidden, unreached peoples.

A Passion for Justice

Roberto could best be described as a man of passion. I met him at a university campus in Brazil.

A confirmed Marxist, he believed in the rights and dignity of all people. His life was energetically and sacrificially committed to championing the cause of the underdog and the oppressed. He was willing to endure what seemed like any amount of hardship towards this end.

He was equally opposed to Christianity.

To him, Christianity was a rich, oppressive system that kept the poor poor and the rich rich. In his eyes, the United States, a "Christian" nation, exploited foreign lands and people for its own interests. "How could six percent of the world's population consume 35 percent of its resources?!" he asked me one day. His concern for people, though definitely in line with biblical values, led him away from Christianity.

Even though Roberto knew more about Christianity than a lot of Christians, he remained trapped—separated from Christ's love because his world convinced him of the evil of Christianity.

Marxist doctrines taught Roberto that religion is the "opiate of the people," that is, it keeps them satisfied with the status quo, willing to endure any amount of economic abuse because they are convinced they have religious significance. Roberto was convinced that religious leaders intentionally manipulate people.

His own dilemma entrenched him in his Marxist viewpoint all the more. Roberto was caught in an economic crunch that made everything outside of his grasp attractive. His only hope for advancement was through education, but the university system in Brazil can only accomodate one out of every 30 applicants. His personal frustrations only reinforced Roberto's belief that Marxism needs to conquer the world.

Roberto, trapped in a system that seeks the extinction of Christianity, will only be reached with the love of Christ if people make specific attempts to step inside his world and his life and show him that Christ is the true liberator—the only one who will ultimately bring justice to all the world. Christians who believe and live this sort of life will cause Roberto's secure ideological cage to crumble.

My few short encounters with him were not enough.

Drugs and Death, His Karma

Three other encounters have taught me about God's love for those beyond the current reaches of the church—those who live in a world with no knowledge of Christ until a Christian steps into that world.

One remains nameless to me.

I almost stumbled over his body as he lay in a street gutter in Calcutta. He wore a dirty, ragged loincloth that only partially covered him. From time to time someone on that crowded sidewalk would accidentally kick him, just as they kicked the debris scattered around him.

But he was oblivious to everything and everybody as he lay there drawing on his opium pipe. Deep pity twisted my stomach and almost overwhelmed me as I realized he was lying there because he was trapped in a religious system that said his life was destined to be just so. The endless crowds of people walking over his body lived by the same philosophy and therefore could never see his need.

He was Hindu and accepted his plight as outside of his control. He simply received the punishment due to him because of deeds he committed in past lives. The thought of escaping his karma or "lot" would never occur to him.

No doubt he was buried later that week, along with several hundred others. The municipal garbage collectors would have found his body and unceremoniously removed it along with all of the other garbage.   One less sidewalk person in a city of 11 million people.

And so it will continue, unless intentional steps are taken to introduce them to a God who forgives, who loves them personally, who offers hope of a new order, who can free people from their karma.

How Can They Hear?

Where the Peruvian Andes slope down to the jungle lies a coffee plantation town called Santa Virginia.   Getting there across the Andes involves a strenuous three-day trek on horseback.

Climb a ridge for half a day, and climb down to a deep river gorge on the other side.   Partially climb to a high plain and camp for the night.   We passed 16,000 feet at one point.   We spent much of those three days in driving cold rainstorms.   Our bodies went almost completely numb, and we thanked God for our rubber-coated ponchos.   We broke ice off small pools of water to wash our faces in the morning and to cook oatmeal for our breakfast.

The plantation was run by Carlos, a steward for an absentee landlord.   Carlos had recently become a Christian and wanted his "pueblo" to hear about Christ.   He asked me to come preach to his people.

When we got to Santa Virginia, it seemed the people were trapped in a time capsule.   Special effort and physical suffering were part of crossing the barriers to reach them.   Here for two weeks, I taught and preached, morning, noon and night.

I noticed that the women rarely attended any of the meetings.   After trying to talk to some of them over meals, I realized they couldn't understand me. Spanish was the trade language—something only the men—who had to deal with outsiders—knew. Their language was a dialect of Quechua. They were separated from Christ by more than rough mountain trails.

We were able to arrange for makeshift translation, and for the first time these women heard the good news. They no longer strained to understand a language as unfamiliar as the face of the one speaking. And before we left, some were able to celebrate the Lord's Supper with us.

Revelation 7:9 was coming true before my eyes. "And there before me was a great multitude that no one could count, from every nation, tribe, people and language!"

Keep Your White God

Andrew is the last teacher I want to mention.

I met him in Westerly, a little town in the Republic of South Africa. It was a place relegated to the "nonwhites," as the South African government calls them. White is the government's standard for rating everyone. People are either white and privileged, or not.

Andrew was black.

I was telling him and a circle of his friends that God loved them deeply and wanted them to experience complete forgiveness. I explained that Jesus had gone to the point of death on the cross for them.

Their response was, "Your God is a white God, and we want nothing to do with him."

I knew too well what they were talking about.

The South African government's policy of racial segregation really means, "Let's keep the best of this country protected for us whites!" The government actually claims that God gave the whites that mandate—to take over the land and rule it. And the largest Christian denomination in South Africa is the main proponent of that policy.

No wonder Andrew was unable to receive the gospel. He was trapped in a cage that tells him that Christianity is the religion of the white man which justifies his deeds of racial and economic oppression. The idea of being a part of that religious tradition is incomprehensible to Andrew.

Andrew and his friends need Christians who will reach inside their world and love them with their very lives, demonstrating the gospel that treats all human beings equally and with dignity. I told him of my disgust for such white twisting of the Bible. But that short evening was not enough to convince him.

CHAPTER TWO

What to Do?

I remember very clearly my own reaction to these needs the first time I encountered them. It was obvious to me as I read the Bible that God intended us to be involved with his world.

My favorite passage in Scripture at the time was a promise from Philippians. Paul reasons with the reader that it would seem to make sense that he should just go straight to heaven. Why not? He was saved from hell and ultimately salvation is being with God.

But he concluded that he had a job to do on earth. And since that was the case, he says, then he could count on having fruitful labor. He didn't say he'd just have something to do, but something fruitful.

I claimed that promise.

Going for Broke

After a while I found myself asking, "If I can make my life fruitful for God eight hours a day, why not 24 hours a day?"

I set out to eradicate my need for sleep. The logic seemed flawless to me—if God wants to use me fruitfully, why shouldn't I give him every minute of my life? That would mean all the more accomplished. And God being who he is, it would be no problem for him to help me exist without sleep.

There was just one flaw in my logic: I am a human being; that's the way God created me. Human beings have to sleep—it's as simple as that.

Well, I slowly reduced my sleeping hours until I was down to three or four hours per day. Every now and then I'd rest my head for a quick 10-minute nap. I had read somewhere that one prominent woman leader had so mastered the art of 10-minute naps that you could talk to her, thinking you had her full attention, and she would actually be in the middle of a short siesta!

So, less sleep.

The next step in my logic called for reducing my spending so that the dollars could go farther in reaching others. I decided to eat one meal per day: peanut butter and jelly sandwiches with coffee. Not the greatest nutrition, but I didn't know any better.

After a while my brain began to feel like scrambled eggs. Lectures at college didn't seem all that coherent. I felt generally "decentralized." But at the same time I was managing to influence several peers to throw their lives into reaching others.

One day a well-meaning friend looked at me and suggested that what I needed was exercise. Peanut butter hadn't left me with the healthiest looking frame or skin tone.

Since I had run cross-country in high school, my mind immediately responded—as jumbled as it was. I decided to begin a rigorous schedule of running the next day, 5 a.m.

I collapsed at the end of the second mile and spent the next two months flat on my back! (I discovered I had mononucleosis.)

I watched a lot of college friends struggle to adjust

their lives to the needs of the world.

Dave was particularly burdened for the hungry. We walked through the Tijuana dump one day. People lived off the throw-aways of others. People suffered from malnutrition and brain damage because they didn't have enough food and water. Dave and I agonized together with a family whose father had just died from complications that grew out of poverty. We stood with the family, looking at the body of a man who died from lack of basic resources while just 20 miles away, across the U.S. border, people suffered from having too much.

Back at school, Dave disappeared for three days. There was no trace of him. Finally, he emerged—from under his bed. He had spent those three days lying on the floor agonizing over the pain that others go through.

Running from the Tension

Cath spent a semester in the inner city being exposed to needs that almost tore her apart. Her upbringing had never let her see that world.

We sat together on the beach talking about her experiences. She had come to the conclusion that the American dream was an offense to God in that it walked over the impoverished. We talked late into the night, as the waves pounded against the shore, wondering what she should do next with her life.

I agreed with her that the churches and Christians around us just didn't seem to have it together. Why weren't they concerned? How could they live in such luxury? What Bible were they reading? But I couldn't tell Cath what to do and I missed her real need of the moment.

She didn't opt for the American dream—her conscience wouldn't let her. But she didn't do much more than "didn't." Cath moved to the Colorado Rockies to take on the life of a hermit. She was unable to resolve the tension of a hurting world and an unresponsive church.

In Search of Reality

And then there was Al.

He joined me on a short work trip to a Mexican orphanage that was badly in need of a sewer system. The kids were in danger of crippling diseases caused by improper sanitation.

Al was sincerely perplexed by the obvious needs that surrounded him at the orphanage. But he couldn't do anything about them. He had to "synthesize!" While the rest of us sweated under the hot Mexican sun, pulling out boulders, fighting tree roots and picking at cement-strong ground, Al spent his time atop one of our dirt piles reasoning aloud about the nature of "reality." It took a good amount of self-control not to chase him into the mountains.

Finally, Al told me that he needed exposure to "real poverty." His request: show me people who are "totally impoverished." I was reluctant to take him somewhere as a tourist, but I said that if exposure would help him do something about what he saw, I'd take him.

The needs we showed him were pitiful.

And he was grateful for this exposure. His journey was now complete. Al slipped into a strange satisfaction that turned into complacency. He had "identified" with the poor, whatever that's supposed to mean, and he could relate his experience to others.

Turning Around

I first met Ted at a college party. He was walking around with the prettiest freshman on his arm, introducing himself as "Frank" and belittling the insecure freshman boys.

Jock and jerk were my impressions of him as I got to know him. A true loser, an insensitive brute, a bigmouthed, obnoxious, overgrown kid.

But Ted's reaction to a missions conference surprised me completely. He saw a clear picture of the world's needs and concluded that he needed to be a part of the solution. He very quickly made plans for a short term mission trip and came back resolved to give his life to missions—even though he had a tough summer.

He has since taken solid steps in missionary preparation, signed up with a mission board, and before long will be working to plant a church among Muslims.

I saw Dan turn around, too.

We used to have a lot of laughs together over coffee—but one day Dan got angry at me for suggesting that a church had to demonstrate beyond a doubt that sinking money into a building program was actually going to advance the spread of the good news. As a pastor's son, Dan grew up measuring the success of a church by the size of the building program or budget.

It only took a few, short cross-cultural trips to see a change in Dan. His heart very quickly softened, and he let go of his assumptions about the church.

Recently I saw Dan in a church pulpit announcing that he was going to let his life count for those that live outside the reaches of the church's love. He challenged the church members to do the same. Currently he's travelling around the U.S. influencing others to join him. He wants to take 1,000 people with him to the mission field.

So how do we respond? What do we do about a hurting world?

You can get overwhelmed and hide under your bed or escape to the mountains. Or you can forget you're human and try to go without food and sleep. But neither response will have a lasting impact on the needy of the world.

Paul was assured of a life of fruitful service, and we can be, too, under Christ's Lordship. It might mean bucking the tide of our culture, and even of the church, but God wants to use our lives. Let's take a look at the terrain ahead of us, through the life of someone who had a tough time understanding what God wanted him to do.

CHAPTER THREE

Jonah Misses the Point

Jonah wasn't a prophet because of something special about him—he was simply a channel that God chose to speak through.

I imagine Jonah had a fairly ordinary life before God called him. He no doubt was proud to be an Israelite, rejoicing that his people had been blessed by God.

As a nation, Israel at that time looked on other nations with scorn—viewing them as unholy blemishes that dishonored the name of God. It was true that the nations did things that God abhored, but Israel had missed the point. They only knew God because of his grace toward them—not because they were special. And God had made it clear that he wanted to show that same grace to other nations.

Of all the peoples around them, there was probably none Israel despised more than Ninevah. Ninevah was notorious because its people boasted of their evil. They even stacked the heads of those they conquered into high mounds as a gruesome display of their violence.

Jonah may well have spent time chatting with his friends about the evil of Ninevah and the doom that ought to fall on that wicked city. But can you imagine what Jonah felt when God told him to bring a message to the Ninevites? "Tell them that unless they repent in

40 days I will destroy them." Jonah loved the idea of
Ninevah's destruction.   Fire and brimstone—that's
what they deserved.

We all know Jonah decided to disobey. But there's
more to the story than that.   Jonah's disobedience
wasn't just plain stubbornness.

Jonah didn't run away because he was afraid of the
Ninevites—vicious as he knew them to be. He didn't
mind being thrown overboard—he knew he was guilty,
but he seemed more willing to die than to do what was
right. He still thought he could thwart God's plans by
ignoring his command.

Inside the whale, Jonah got a chance to reflect on
God's goodness to him.

You brought my life up from the pit,
O Lord my God. . .
Those who cling to worthless idols
forfeit the grace that could be theirs (2:6,8).

Thoroughly grateful for his salvation, Jonah got a
boost back to shore.

He still wasn't eager to go to Ninevah, but he didn't
dare disobey God again. He went, but not out of love
for the Ninevites. After marching through the city for
three days, Jonah sat back to watch the flames come
down from heaven to devour those wretched people.

To Jonah's great surprise, Ninevah repented. He
warned them, but he didn't expect them to change. He
didn't offer any guidance on *how* to repent. They had
to guess, as the king's decree reflects.

Let everyone call urgently on God. Let them give up
their evil ways and their violence. Who knows? God
may yet relent and with compassion turn from his
fierce anger, so that we will not perish (3:8-9).

Jonah's response to the repentance of Ninevah

gives us a clue as to why he disobeyed in the first place. Instead of rejoicing as the city turned to the Lord, Jonah complained. He argued with God:

"Is this not what I said when I was still at home? That is why I was so quick to flee to Tarshish. I knew that you are a gracious and compassionate God, slow to anger and abounding in love, a God who relents from sending calamity" (4:2).

Jonah knew God was merciful. That's exactly what he feared. He didn't want the Ninevites to have a chance to repent. They deserved destruction. Jonah didn't understand what God was trying to do through Israel's entire history. Jonah had missed all the clues that God loved all the nations. Israel wasn't the *only* people God loved; they were supposed to be a part of God's purpose to bless and redeem all peoples.

The last words of Jonah recorded in Scripture are: "I am angry enough to die" (4:9).

Jonah wasn't alone. Through most of Israel's history, God's people preferred to keep his blessing to themselves. The result, as we can see in Jonah, was a selfish, disobedient heart—one that hoarded the grace of God and refused to rejoice when other nations repented.

Israel was to bring the Messiah into the world, and when he came, he found his people still following in Jonah's footsteps.

CHAPTER FOUR

Jesus Makes It Final

Jonah was fuzzy about his role as an Israelite; Jesus was absolutely clear about his role as the Messiah of the nations.

Throughout his ministry, Jesus showed his love for people of many different nations. Again and again, he challenged the contemporary belief that God loved only the Jews. Jesus brought his earthly ministry to a climax in Jerusalem, the focal point of Israel's national pride. There he condemned his people's selfishness and unmistakably opened the way for all peoples to receive God's grace.

By the time he reached Jerusalem, he had gathered quite a large following. People had been healed, raised from the dead, and forgiven. Many hoped he would be their ruler and political leader. And others worshiped him as the Messiah.

He entered the city knowing he would die there. His life was about to culminate in a scene that would be the most exquisite combination of horror and compassion. Mere men would take the King of the universe and hold his arms against the wood as they drove big spikes through his hands. He would die as a criminal before a jeering public.

But only because he allowed it. He had given up everything, humbled himself and become a servant to the point of death in order to rescue us with his love.

He created us from dust; he could simply have left us alone, but he chose instead to give himself to redeem the world.

The people welcomed him into Jerusalem as a King. They cheered and covered his path with cloaks and palm branches.

"Hosanna to the Son of David.

Blessed is He who comes in the name of the Lord! Hosanna in the Highest" (Matthew 21:9).

"Hosanna!" "Save!" This must have been a bittersweet moment for Jesus. The people of Israel had had a special relationship with him since Abraham. They had known him as protector, deliverer, Father and King, and they looked forward to the Messiah's coming. And now, 2,000 years after Abraham, he looked at them with pity, as sheep without a shepherd—people who somehow missed the King of love. Earlier, Jesus had looked over the city of Jerusalem and said, "How often I have longed to gather your children together, as a hen gathers her chicks under her wings, but you were not willing" (Luke 13:34).

Then he entered the temple courtyard. The heart that was filled with compassion for the lost erupted with the anger of God himself as Jesus saw the Israelites participate in the ultimate deed of defiance.

Was he angry over a bake sale?

No. He singlehandedly cleared the temple courtyard, driving people out, overturning tables, scattering money, freeing animals. And he shouted at the people:

"My house will be a house of prayer for all the nations, but you have made it a den of robbers!" (Luke 19:40).

Jesus was quoting a passage in Isaiah 56 that proclaimed that his salvation was meant for everyone, and that his temple was to be a center of worship for people from every nation.

God had given the Israelites very specific instructions in the design of the temple to make a courtyard for the Gentiles—as a place where people of other nations could come to worship the Messiah. They had turned this courtyard into a marketplace. In effect, they were keeping the nations out. They were following in the grand tradition of Jonah.

It is Finished

A few days later Jesus made his purpose for coming to earth absolutely clear as he hung on the cross.

As his life slipped away, he screamed in what must have been both triumph and agony, "It is finished!" At that moment, the curtain that barred any but the High Priest from the Holy of Holies in the temple was torn in two from top to bottom.

The message was clear. The priests weren't the only ones to have access to God's presence. They had been furious at Jesus for clearing the temple. In fact, they plotted to have him killed. And then the great curtain was split as if by the hands of God—right before their eyes. Anyone could enter the Holy of Holies—the place where God's presence dwelt on earth. Anyone could freely receive salvation. The Jews were no longer the sole stewards of the grace of God.

Jesus had explained to the disciples earlier (though I'm certain they didn't fully understand) that his death would accomplish this.

Some Greeks had come to Jerusalem for the Passover feast. They wanted to see Jesus. Jesus took the opportunity to remind the disciples again that he would die soon, and he told them that his death would bring salvation to all.

"The hour has come for the Son of Man to be glorified. I tell you the truth, unless a kernel of wheat falls into the ground and dies, it remains only a single seed. But if it dies, it produces many seeds.... But when I am lifted up, I will draw all men to myself" (John 12:23-24, 32).

The text explains that Jesus was referring to being crucified—he would be lifted up on a cross in order that all people might come to him.

Jonah Revisited

Before Jesus entered Jerusalem and cleared the temple, some of the Pharisees had asked him for a miraculous sign—something that would give them some assurance of who he was. Jesus' response was very direct:

"A wicked and adulterous generation asks for a miraculous sign! But none will be given except the sign of the prophet Jonah. For as Jonah was three days and three nights in the belly of a huge fish, so the Son of Man will be three days and three nights in the heart of the earth. The men of Ninevah will stand up at the judgement with this generation and condemn it; for they repented at the preaching of Jonah, and now one greater than Jonah is here (Matt 12:34-41).

The message is stunningly clear! The people you rejected, whom you refused to show my grace, did repent. Jonah's very weak call to repentance was enough for them.

"I'm much greater than Jonah," explains Jesus.

"You have sufficient sign to repent. And if you don't, you will be judged by the Ninevites themselves!"

Jonah had been fuzzy about his role, but Jesus was absolutely clear—he was the Savior of all peoples.

CHAPTER FIVE

Where No Man Has Gone Before

Paul had an ambition. It dominated his life and gave direction to everything he did. He knew what his life was for—and what it wasn't for. In stark contrast to Jonah, Paul had no fuzziness in his mind about where he was going.

He expressed his ambition in many ways, but probably most clearly in a letter to some Christians that he was hoping to meet soon.

I have made it my ambition to evangelize not where Christ was already named that I might not build on the foundation of another, but as it is written, "They who had no news of him shall see and they who have not heard shall understand" (Romans 15:20-21, author's translation).

Paul's ambition focused his life and gave him a criterion for evaluating the opportunities that came his way. He was determined to avoid two activities: 1) going where Christ was named, and 2) building foundations where they already existed. Let's explore both of these.

Building Foundations

"I thought Paul was a tentmaker," you might say. "What is he doing laying foundations?" In another letter, Paul calls himself a "wise master builder" (I Corinthians 3:10). As the architect and general contractor, he says that he "laid a foundation and another is building on it."

The foundation in this passage was the first beginnings of the spiritual fellowship at Corinth, the first church in that region. Paul saw his role as a church starter, putting together the beginnings of a church where there were none. He seemed to be happy to let others build up the church after he left. He cared about every church that he planted (II Corinthians 11:25), but in most cases, he left it to others to bring the church to maturity.

Once Paul got started from Antioch on his missionary journeys, he never again limited his ministry to one place for very long. He always moved on, laying more foundations where there weren't any.

That's what he was explaining to his friends in Rome. He knew a lot of people in the Roman church, as we can see from his greetings in chapter 16. He had long intended to visit them, but he got held up. Why? His ambition got in the way of what would have been a happy visit.

Those who were not told about [Jesus] will see, and those who have not heard will understand. This is why I have often been hindered from coming to you (Romans 15:21-22).

A church at Rome was already well established. No foundation laying was needed, so he had passed up several opportunities to visit them. The only way he could justify a visit was the prospect of going through Rome on his way to Spain—where there was no gospel witness and no church at the time.

Paul didn't let himself get sidetracked, let alone run away from where God was sending him, as Jonah had.

Naming Christ

Another thing Paul didn't want to do: to go where Christ was named. As he struggled to lay new foundations, Paul made sure he was working where Christ was not named.

What does it mean to "name Christ?" Naming Christ is more than shouting the words, "Jesus Christ" from the rooftops or street corners. It is making him known for who he is. For Jesus to be named is for him to be recognized as the Messiah (that's what "Christ" means)—the One who forgives sins, frees from Satanic bondage, rescues from hell, liberates the oppressed, restores society, and heals minds, lives and families. In short, only Jesus is Lord.

But Jesus can only be known as Messiah and Lord through people who live out his Lordship. Christ is "named" by believers who reflect his character and do his work. It is no coincidence that the followers of Jesus came to be called "Christians" or "Christ people" by the watching world. It's through his people that God has a name in the world.

Why would Paul want to go where Christ was not named? It's pretty clear—his job was to make Christ known to cultures or nations for the first time. If God's work in revealing the saving kingship of Jesus was already underway in a certain place, Paul quickly moved on to see the Lordship of Jesus explode into life in another place.

Naming Christ and laying foundations go hand in hand. They both refer to the initial church starting (or church planting, as some call it) among a people who have not yet experienced the redeeming kingdom rule of Jesus. Where Paul had already done this, he could say, "I have fulfilled the gospel of Christ" (Romans

15:19).

This was the driving goal of Paul's life, not just to be involved in gospel work, or to have a ministry, or to maximize his spiritual gifts, or to use his college major, but somehow to *fulfill* the gospel—to see Christ's name spread everywhere.

He was motivated and empowered by the Bible's assurance that everyone would hear. In fact, he quotes a promise from Isaiah to help explain his ambition:

They who had no news of him shall see and they who have not heard shall understand (52:15).

Paul was striving to make the love and lordship of Jesus known where he wasn't known, visible where he wasn't seen, and comprehended where he was not yet understood.

Look again at the verse Paul chose to back up his life ambition. It's just a verse from Isaiah. It's not a direct command like "Go make the Messiah known." It's a simple promise about what God will do in the world. You would think that Paul would have quoted Jesus' command to preach the gospel to everyone. But he didn't. He set his life goals on a broader base than one verse. He lined his ambition up with the whole Bible.

This business of names and foundations started a long time ago. And Paul was conscious of the whole flow of the biblical story. He saw himself as part of that same story! Unlike Jonah, Israel, the Pharisees and the temple priests, Paul realized that at the heart of God lies a passion to bring his love to all the nations.

Let's flash back to the beginning of the story to take a closer look at what Jonah and his friends missed. God has made his passion clear from the very beginning.

CHAPTER SIX

A Blessing to All Nations

Right at the beginning of Scripture, shortly after the accounts of the fall, the flood and the tower of Babel, God visited a man called Abram. He gave Abram a strange command and some amazing promises.

"Leave your country, your people and your father's household and go to the land I will show you.

I will make you into a great nation and I will bless you;

I will make your name great and you will be a blessing.

I will bless those who bless you, and whoever curses you I will curse; and all peoples on earth will be blessed through you" (Genesis 12:1-3).

Many Christians through the years have had a great deal of respect for Israel, and rightly so—being made into a great nation by God, from the beginning of history, is no small thing. But all too often we miss the whole point of God's singling Israel out. The key to Israel's role in the Old Testament world is given at the end of verse three: "... and all peoples on earth will be blessed through you."

God chose Israel as a channel of his blessing. In his desire to reach the whole world with his love, God chose Israel, blessed it, and made it a standard of righteousness to show the other nations that the Lord is the only true God.

Much like Mary, the mother of Jesus, Israel simply acted as a *channel through which* the Messiah, the Savior, was presented to the nations. Israel wasn't great because of the number of people or the wars it won or the cities it built—Israel was great because God called the nation to demonstrate his character and love to the nations around it.

From Genesis to Revelation, God's strategy for winning the nations shows up again and again. In the Old Testament, God chose to bring his salvation to the nations primarily through Israel. In the New Testament, he works through a "new Israel"—the Church. After the death and resurrection of Christ, Christians are God's channels of blessing to the nations.

Spread It Around!

There were many ways that God worked through Israel. Israel demonstrated its special relationship with God in its political structure and relations with other nations. Israel was the only nation ever called to represent God as a political body. The law given to Moses ordered every facet of life.

Israel's king was God. The other nations had their kings and gods too. When Israel went to war, the battle was between the *God of Israel* and the ruler of the other nation. And if Israel won the battle, it proved that its God was superior.

When Israel was meticulously obedient to God, not one of its soldiers would be wounded. Thousands of the enemy's men would die or surrender, but there was not a soldier scathed from the army of the Hebrew God! The other nations took note!

But whenever Israel sinned or chose to do things its way, it suffered injuries and even defeat. It was obvious, especially to the other nations, *who* was behind Israel's victories.

Israel was to demonstrate the love of God as well as his power by showing hospitality and kindness to strangers and outcasts. Throughout Scripture, God emphasized his concern for these people.

Do not mistreat an alien or oppress him (Exodus 22:21).

The alien living among you must be treated as one of your native-born. Love him as yourself, for you were aliens in Egypt. I am the Lord your God (Leviticus 19:34).

Cursed is the man who withholds justice from the alien, the fatherless or the widow (Deuteronomy 27:19).

Other nations would be attracted to this strange Hebrew God who *demanded* that kindness be shown to the alien.

As they lived out God's love and justice and power, Israel would reveal the *name* of their God to the nations around them.

"What's in a name?" you might ask. Well, let's see what God says about his name:

"I will cause all my goodness to pass in front of you, and I will proclaim *my name, the Lord,* in your presence.... And he passed in front of Moses, proclaiming, "The Lord, the Lord, the compassionate and gracious God, slow to anger, abounding in love and faithfulness, maintaining love to thousands, and forgiving wickedness, rebellion and sin. Yet he does not leave the guilty unpunished. . . (Exodus 33:19; 34:6-7).

These were the Lord's words to Moses on Mount Sinai. This God was totally unlike the gods of the other nations. Israel was to present that Name to the nations. The goodness of God was "good news" for the nations.

A Blessing to the Nations

Even Abram, the one God gave the promise to, had to be reminded again and again that God really would make him into a great nation and bless the world through him. God brought him through years of testing to prepare him to be that blessing.

Abram's first struggles of faith came as he grew older and didn't yet have a son. How could he ever be the father of a great nation?

The Lord came and repeated his promise. He didn't immediately give Abram a son, but instead demonstrated the seriousness of his promise. He had Abram get a heifer, a goat, a ram, a pigeon and a dove. Abram cut the animals in half and separated the carcasses. A blazing torch appeared and passed between the halves.

This was a customary way of making very serious promises. It meant, "May what happened to these animals happen to me if I don't keep my word." And God repeated his promise that Abram's descendants would possess the land.

A few years later, when Abram was 99 and still without an heir, God prepared him further for the great role he would play in blessing the nations. God changed his name to *Abraham*, "for I have made you the father of many nations" (Genesis 17:5).

Even before the birth of Isaac, Abraham got a taste of what Israel's role before God would be. God told him that Sodom and Gomorrah were about to be judged for their sin, and he gave Abraham a chance to intercede for those cities. Scripture makes it clear that this too was part of God's long-range plan for Abraham and his descendants.

"Shall I hide from Abraham what I am about to do? Abraham will surely become a great and powerful nation, and all nations on earth will be blessed through him" (Genesis 18:17-18).

There was one more test in store for Abraham— one more opportunity to make sure he understood God's purposes. God told Abraham to take his son Isaac up the mountain and offer him as a burnt sacrifice.

You might expect Abraham to shout: "Give me a break, will you?" But by this time he fully trusted that God would make him a channel of blessing to the nations—even if he didn't understand how. So he went up the mountain, built the altar, arranged the wood and was about to plunge the knife into his son's chest when God stopped him. The Lord couldn't conceal his joy from Abraham:

"I swear by myself. . . through your offspring all nations on earth will be blessed, because you have obeyed me"(Genesis 22:16,18).

The Old Testament Thread

The promise was repeated not only to Isaac and Jacob, but over and over to Israel throughout the Old Testament.

The Psalms expressed the heights of Israel's worship, and they are full of references to the nations worshiping God, too.

Among the gods there is none like you, O Lord. . .
All the nations you have made will come and worship before you, O Lord; And they will *bring glory to your*

name (Psalm 86:8-9).

All the ends of the earth will remember and turn to the Lord,and *all the families of the nations* will bow down before him. . . (Psalm 22:27).

Shout with joy to God, *all the earth*Sing to *the glory of His name*. . . So great is your power that your enemies cringe before you *All the earth* bows down to you. . . they *sing praise to you*. . . (Psalm 66:1-4).

The following blessing might sound familiar to you from church, but look at the whole Psalm.

May God be gracious to us and bless us and make his face shine upon us; may your ways be known on earth, your salvation among all nations.

May the peoples praise you, O God; may all the peoples praise you. May the nations be glad and sing for joy, for you rule the peoples justly and guide the nations of the earth. May the peoples praise you, O God; may all the peoples praise you.

Then the land will yield its harvest, and God, our God, will bless us. God will bless us, and all the ends of the earth will fear him (Psalm 67).

The prophets called Israel to remember its purpose as a nation. And when Israel's disobedience got in the way of the nations' knowing God, the prophets made it clear that God would bless the nations as he had promised.

Therefore, say to the house of Israel, "This is what the Sovereign Lord says: It is not for your sake, O house of Israel, that I am going to do these things, but for the sake of *my holy name*, which you have profaned among the nations where you have gone. And I will show the holiness of my great name, which has been profaned among the nations, the name you have profaned among them. *Then the* nations will know that I am the Lord," declares the Sovereign Lord, "when I show myself holy through you before their eyes" (Ezekiel 36:22-23).

Revival in Israel was to extend to the nations:

I will cleanse [Israel] from all the sin which they have committed against me and will forgive all their sins of rebellion against me. Then this city will bring me renown, joy, praise and honor *before all the nations on earth* that hear of all the good things I do for it; and they will be in awe and tremble at the abundant prosperity and peace I will provide for it (Jeremiah 33:8-9).

The Messiah was promised, not only as Israel's King, but as the Savior and King of the nations.

Here is my servant, whom I uphold, my chosen one in whom I delight; I will put my spirit on him *and he will bring justice to the nations. He will not falter or be discouraged, till he establishes justice on earth.* In his law the islands will put their hope (Isaiah 42:1,4). In my vision at night I looked, and there before me was one like a son of man, coming with the clouds of heaven. He approached the Ancient of Days and was led into his presence. He was given authority, glory and soverign power; *all peoples, nations and men of every language worshiped him.* His dominion is an everlasting dominion that will not pass away and his kingdom is one that will never be destroyed (Daniel 7:13-14).

Back to the Temple

Remember how Jesus cleared out the temple because of the abuse of the Gentile courtyard?

When Solomon dedicated the temple he prayed a long prayer. His prayer dealt with two areas: how the temple would be a source of cleansing and healing for *individuals* and how it would be a blessing to the *nations*. In fact, the former is a means of ensuring the latter.

As for *the foreigner who does not belong to your people Israel* but has come from a distant land because of your name—for men will hear of your great name and your mighty hand and your outstretched arm— when he comes and prays toward this temple, then hear from heaven, your dwelling place, and do whatever the foreigner asks of you so that all the peoples of the earth may know your name and fear you. . . and may know that this house I have built bears your name. And may these words of mine which I have prayed before the Lord, be near to the Lord our God day and night, that he may uphold the cause of his servant and the cause of his people Israel according to each day's need, so that *all of the peoples of the earth may know that the Lord is God and that there is no other* (I Kings 8:41-43, 59-60).

Loving Other Nations

The Old Testament is full of stories of individuals who demonstrated the love of God by touching the lives of people from other nations. Here are just a few examples:

- Abraham intercedes for Sodom and Gomorrah (Genesis 18).
- Joseph saves thousands of Egyptians and other surrounding nations from starvation (Genesis 41).
- Joshua spares Rahab and her Canaanite family (Joshua 2, 6:22-23).
- Naomi is a blessing to Ruth, a Moabite (Ruth).

- Solomon shares his wisdom with Sheba, an Arabian (I Kings 10).
- Elisha heals Naaman, a Syrian soldier (2 Kings 5).
- Daniel witnesses to the kings of Babylon and Persia (Daniel).

But the sad fact remains that the net actions of the nation of Israel were a big negative. People who reached out to other nations were the exception rather than the rule. Old Jonah was typical of Israel's attitude.

Israel never forgot that they were a chosen people—unfortunately, they forgot what they were chosen to do. The call to bless the nations runs all through Scripture, yet the Jews kept missing it. Perhaps it was this tragic failure of his people that Jesus wept over as he looked out over Jerusalem.

Fortunately, God's faithfulness does not depend on ours. Even Jonah remembered the words God used to describe his name to Moses on Mount Sinai: "Compassionate and gracious, slow to anger, abounding in lovingkindness and truth" (Jonah 4:2). In the New Testament, God turned the Old Testament's story of failure around.

CHAPTER SEVEN

Mixed Blood

Have you ever wondered why the New Testament starts with a genealogy? It's not a "grabber" introduction, but look again—it's all about God's faithfulness.

Ray Bakke, a specialist in urban missions, offers some insights on this first chapter of Matthew. He said it so well, I'm just going to excerpt part of a recent talk he gave.

Cemetery Tour

The good news begins with a list of dead people. It is like a cemetery tour in which Matthew says, "So-and-so begat so-and-so begat so-and-so." But in those first six verses, four women are mentioned among the fourteen names. You are probably well aware of them. They are Tamar from Genesis 38, Rahab from Joshua 2, Ruth, and "Mrs. Uriah," the wife of Uriah, who is, of course, Bathsheba. I call them the skeletons in the closet or the "other women in the family of Jesus." The fact that they are mentioned in the opening paragraph of the New Testament and that the whole thing is labeled "Good News" should grab our attention.

There is quite a history of interpretation of the passage. Jerome, one of the great classical interpreters of the Scripture, looked at those four names and said, "I think these women were all sinners and that this passage, therefore, is about *grace.*" We don't know that Ruth was a sinner in such a public way as the others were, but as a Moabite, she was part of a sinful *culture.* (Moab was the offspring of Lot's incestuous relationship with his daughter.)   So Jerome said that these four women were sinners. The good news is that the grace of God saves people like this.

Luther looked at those four women and saw something else. He saw that all four were foreigners. Tamar and Rahab were Canaanite women. Luther remembered the curse on Canaan from Genesis 9 and said that the cursed race had been included in the salvation of Jesus. The Canaanites had been "choreographed," as it were, into the godly, redemptive line.

Luther also noticed that Ruth was a Moabite and Mrs. Uriah presumably a Hittite, and so he said that while Jerome is correct, the passage is about grace and the gospel, grace comes from the *outside* and grace is *redemptive.* Also, said Luther, this passage is about missions. That is, it is not just the sinners who are saved, it's *foreign* sinners who are saved. In the 28th chapter of Matthew we are told to go into all the world and preach the gospel, but a list of names in chapter one tells *who* all the world is: Canaanites, Moabites, Hittites and the Jews. And so you have a list of names in a stylized genealogy which lets us know that Matthew's purpose is *missionary* right from the start.

Matthew clearly is picking up themes that occur all through the book, and deliberately choosing names in the three sets of fourteen to summarize Israel's history that have theological purposes, not just biological ones. All you have to do is take the genealogy of Matthew 1 and compare it with the one in Exodus 6 and the one in the first chapters of Chronicles, and you will see a lot of differences. It is not that they are inaccurate, but that the Hebrew has no word for grandson. "Jesus Christ, son of David, son of Abraham" has a thousand years between each term, so the Hebrew concept of "son" is so elastic that you can choose your descendants to make a theological point. Clearly, Matthew appears to have picked up a missionary theme from the great commission and brought it right back into his little genealogy.

I think there is a third reason why those names were mentioned. Jesus obviously was of mixed blood. If he had mothers from four different racial groups, if in fact he had *Canaanite, Moabite, Hittite, and Jewish ancestry*, then not only did Jesus get his blood from the world, and shed his blood *for* the world, it was *mixed racial blood* that was shed on the cross for the sins of the world. In a time of enormous racism around the world, this is very good news.

Too often Mary has received all the attention, and these other women have been left as skeletons in the closet. I think their inclusion here is very much a part of what the gospel is and for *whom* it is intended. So when you read, "He came unto his own," now you know who his own are: the cursed Canaanites, the incestuous Moabites, and the Hittites—the most warlike race of the ancient world—as well as the Jews. That's what it means to say "He came unto his own."

And so, in the very beginning of the New Testament we have the message presented once again: My salvation is for all the nations.

We saw Jesus' dramatic way of saying it as he cleansed the temple. But this was only part of it. His daily life was a constant witness to the fact that the good news was for all the nations. Skim through the gospels sometime and take a look at all the times Jesus talked with, healed and forgave Gentiles.

So consistent was this message that Jesus could leave his disciples with a parting command, fully trusting they would carry it out.

Untangling the Great Commission

All authority in heaven and on earth has been given to me. Therefore go and make disciples of all nations, baptizing them in the name of the Father, and of the Son and of the Holy Spirit, and teaching them to obey everything I have commanded you. And surely I will be with you always, to the very end of the age (Matthew 28:18-20).

The "great commission," as it has come to be known, is usually seen as the pivotal missions passage. Here God lets us in on the secret that he also intends to reach the rest of the world with his love.

Hopefully, at this point in the book, you are shouting, "That just isn't so! Missions doesn't depend on one passage."

Indeed, the theme of mission is the very *core* of the Bible. It is the skeleton on which hang all the stories, exhortations and history contained between the covers of our Bibles. I've heard the Bible called the love story of Jesus to the whole world.

All that the great commission does is to *sum up* for the disciples what their task is now that the Master is taking off. They've already graduated from Jesus' *three-year* mission class!

Making the great commission the most important mission passage in the Bible is a crime. But so many of our churches have committed a much greater crime than that in the way they *interpret* the great commission.

Such a mess has been made of it that it can mean almost anything from, "Be a good Christian wherever you are," to "You're not really saved completely until you're baptized," to "Jesus will always be with you no matter what your circumstances."

Let's untangle the poor mixed-up thing!

First of all, the key thought is "make disciples of all nations." In the original language, "make disciples" is the only active verb; the others just expand on *where* and *how* to disciple the nations—by going, baptizing and teaching.

This word "disciple" is problem enough. Many Christians and many churches take the word from this verse and state their ministry objective: to make disciples. It doesn't matter who or where—just make disciples and you're obeying the great commission.

Not so! Jesus stated very specifically that we are to disciple *all nations*. The great commission is a command with a global scope—it can't be stripped of this meaning.

It so beautifully sums up the task that the Lord has given to his whole church, the task that forms the core of the Bible: bringing all the nations, the whole world, under his Lordship! This is a mandate that the entire body is meant to accomplish together.

The rest of the great commission is the nuts and bolts of fulfilling the mandate. Let's look at the three parts described by Jesus.

Go: This may seem obvious, but put yourself back in the disciple's shoes. God's redemptive plan began with Israel. As nations were drawn to Israel as a political entity on a specific piece of real estate with a temple at its center, they were drawn to the Messiah.

But now anyone who decided to put full trust in the Messiah became a member of the new Israel—a new people with no land, no earthly government, and no central temple. Their very bodies became temples of the Holy Spirit. Anywhere they went, they would draw people to their Lord. And Jesus told them to go *everywhere*.

Jesus had prepared the disciples to receive these marching orders.

First, Jesus' ministry was always on the move—going to the people. They had followed him everywhere for three years. They knew what he meant when he told an inquirer one day, "Foxes have holes, birds have nests, but the Son of Man has no place to lay His head" (Matthew 8:20).

Second, the city of Jerusalem where Jesus' ministry culminated and where the church got its start was not home. Others considered them outsiders, "hicks" from Galilee. Having pulled up their Galilean roots, they were ready to go.

Baptize: Jesus was looking for people who identified with *his name*. You might say that to become a "believer" is to become a "revealer." This was a means of announcing to themselves and to the world that all the old had passed away—*washed* by the blood—and now the new had come! Baptized Christians gained a completely new identity—the name of Christ.

Remember God revealing his name to Moses on

Mount Sinai? This was the God that Israel was to reveal to the nations, and now the members of the new Israel were given the responsibility of revealing God as *Loving Father, Comforting* and *Power-giving Spirit* and *All-forgiving, Saving Jesus!*

Be baptized in *that* name. Call the nations' attention to *that* Lord.

Teach to obey: Our Western culture has managed to reduce "teaching" to something that happens passively in the classroom, something that is received as notes are taken.

But that isn't the message of Christ. He calls people to follow him with all their hearts, souls, strength and minds. This wasn't a *religion to be studied*, this was a *person to be followed*. He taught obedience, not content. His disciples were to teach, not all there is to know, but readiness to obey all of Jesus' commands.

The disciples understood their task well: Go and call all the nations of the world to live under the Lordship of the Christ, the Father, the Spirit.

Acts is an exciting story. It shows the disciples making their first attempt to move out into all the world with the responsibility and authority given them by Jesus. Some, like Peter, struggled initially with the idea of including all the nations, but by the time the book of Acts wraps up, that band of disciples couldn't be stopped. Their stomping ground was the world, all the nations—nothing less.

History confirms that most of the disciples died a martyr's death in foreign nations. What an amazing and encouraging contrast to the failures of Israel, Jonah, the Pharisees and temple priests! The disciples caught on to what generations of Jews had missed.

A Very Good Ending

The book of Revelation confirms the hope that we start to see in Acts—the fulfillment of the promise to Abraham.

The beginning of chapter seven promises that many from Israel will be in heaven. Then it goes on to reveal a happy sight:

After this I looked and there before me was a great multitude that no one could count, from *every* nation, tribe, people and language, standing before the throne and in front of the Lamb. They were wearing white robes and were holding palm branches in their hands. And they cried out in a loud voice:

Salvation belongs to our God
Who sits on the throne,
And to the Lamb.

All the angels were standing around the throne and around the elders and the four living creatures.

They fell down on their faces before the throne and worshiped God, saying:

Amen!
Praise and glory
and wisdom and thanks and honor
and power and strength
be to our God for ever and ever.
Amen!

(7:9-12)

The angels couldn't control themselves in this scene. They had watched, as first fellow angels, then man, rebelled and rejected God's goodness. They saw the saga of Israel. They anxiously waited, poised and ready to burst through the sky to hoist Jesus from the cross if he had only given the word.

And now, as earthly time came to a close, they were overcome by the sight of members of *all nations, tribes, tongues and people* worshiping their Lord and Savior.

CHAPTER EIGHT

The Hidden Half

The Bible tells a story of *love*. God loved the world so much that he sent his Son to die for us. Jesus endured persecution, misunderstanding and physical suffering so we could enjoy his salvation. We see God's love in action throughout the Bible as people are healed, fed, forgiven, freed, clothed, redeemed.

The Bible tells a story of *hope*. We're assured of a personal hope that cannot be shaken—the knowledge that we will spend eternity in bliss through God's unbelievable grace to us. Come what may in this life, our future is secure.

But that hope isn't just for us—it's a *global* hope. God's intention throughout history has been to see that hope take root in every nation. And the book of Revelation confirms that hope as we see representatives of every tribe, tongue and nation worshiping God.

The Bible tells a story of *faith*. It is full of the stories of faithful men and women, but most of all, it is the story of God's faithfulness. His determination to draw the nations to himself is as sure as his plan to work through his people. Faithfully he calls and enables; he is patient and slow to anger. Our faithful God never gives up on his people or his world.

The Bible says faith, hope and love are the things that will last forever—the story continues today.

God is on the Move!

Peter Wagner of Pasadena, California, and David Barrett of Nairobi, Kenya, have spent years keeping tabs on the progress of the gospel around the world. Here are some of the things they have discovered.

Every day 78,000 people become Christians. Of those, 21,000 live in Africa and Southeast Asia. Over 1,000 new churches open their doors *every week* in Asia and Africa alone.

In 1900, there were only about fifty thousand Protestants in Latin America. Within 80 years that number jumped to 20 million, and by the end of this century some say there may be up to 100 million Protestants.

Wagner writes about one Latin American church:

One of my favorite churches is the Jotabeche Methodist Pentecostal Church of Santiago, pastored by Javier Vasquez. For years I visited them in their old building on Jotabeche Street which accommodated 5,000 people. But that became entirely inadequate to handle the crowds, so they built a new sanctuary to accommodate 16,000 around the corner on Alameda Avenue. A balcony on one side holds the 2,000 member choir and orchestra combined. On a typical Sunday evening, when the main service is held, 1,000 instruments—mostly guitars, mandolins, and accordions—will be playing while all 2,000 choir members are singing special numbers.

But this building is also inadequate because Vasquez's flock numbers between 80,000 and 90,000 members twelve years of age and over. Members are allowed to attend the mother church only once a month. The other three Sundays they participate in the activities of one of the many smaller "classes" located in the different neighborhoods of the city. The classes are like satellite churches. Their membership runs between 800 and 3,000 and each is led by one of Javier Vasquez's associate pastors.

The story in Africa is similar. There were less than 10 million Christians there in 1900. By 1980 that number had grown to more than 200 million, and by the end of this century it will be around 400 million.

One German missionary in South Africa has such a successful ministry among the blacks that he has a tent that holds 34,000 people. Six semi-trailers are required to transport it to the next meeting point.

Ethiopian Christians have undergone all sorts of persecution since a Marxist government took over in 1975. But persecution has been unable to stop church growth. The Lutheran Mekane Yesus ("Household of Jesus") church, which reported 30,000 members in 1960, grew to 500,000 by 1980! Almost all of those new members were added between 1978 and 1980.

The picture is as bright in Asia. A hundred years ago there were no churches in Korea. Today there are 6,000 in the city of Seoul alone. Korea is famous for the largest gatherings of Christians ever and the largest church in the world. Christian rallies have drawn over 1 million people at three different times—2.7 million people came together on one day in 1980. The Full Gospel Central Church is fast approaching 500,000 members. Over 19,000 home cell groups, each headed by a trained leader, form the dynamic base of this church.

In 1950 China closed its doors and forced all missionaries to leave. The persecution of Christians began then and grew to horrendous proportions during the Cultural Revolution in the 1960's.

Before the revolution, there may have been a million Chinese believers. When foreigners were allowed back into China in the late 1970's, they discovered that the church had flourished during those dark years—some estimate there may be 50 million Christians in China today.

This tremendous story of the growth of the church around the world makes it clear that Christianity is no longer the white man's religion. Today 53 percent of the world's believers are not white.

Our faithful Lord is on the move! But that doesn't mean the job is done. Over half the world remains hidden from the gospel—out of earshot of the good news of the Kingdom, and unfortunately, out of sight of the church.

In order to discover this hidden half, we need to understand our world—the global trends and realities that shape the lives of the billions without Christ. Here are a few of the major factors.

Urban Explosion

The world is becoming a city. From the time of Christ until 1800, less than 3 percent of the world lived in cities. One hundred years later that had grown to 9.2 percent, by 1950 it was 29 percent, and by the year 2000 half the world's people will live in urban areas.

There is no other term for this growth but "explosion." Every month the world sprouts another Chicago. By the year 2000, 10 third world cities will have more than 10 million residents each. Mexico City alone may have 32 million.

This skyrocketing growth is also a ticking population bomb that threatens to turn cities around the world into nightmarish scenes of suffering and despair, characterized by massive unemployment, woefully inadequate food supplies, absolute poverty and ravaged environments.

Refugees

There are more than 10 million refugees in the world today. Few have been uprooted by famines, floods or earthquakes. Nearly all of them are victims of economic exploitation, wars, revolutions or oppression related to religion, nationality, or political identity.

For most refugees, the decision to flee is made on a moment's notice and in an atmosphere of panic or hysteria. Their urgency usually means inadequate preparation—overnight, the goal has simply become survival. Once they start their flight, they face the dangers of being caught, of bad weather, and often of piracy.

Safely reaching a refugee camp only means facing another demoralizing situation. Says Burt Singleton of World Vision, "[The refugee] is segregated from the host population, forced to share needed facilities, embarrassed by lack of privacy. . . within an overcrowed, limited and restricted area." And they wait for a solution—going home if the situation allows, or resettlement in another country.

For most refugees, their exile sets them on a journey that might take most of the rest of their lives. Piecing together their shattered world will require more than a flurry of quick-fix, stop-gap measures.

Today, refugees are found surviving and waiting and trying to make a new life on every continent:

Africa	2,251,600
Asia	954,700
Europe	613,200
Latin America	388,700
Middle East	4,637,200
North America	1,187,000
Total	10,032,400

Prostitution

Prostitution enslaves hundreds of thousands in a dehumanizing system of abuse and oppression. The global dimensions of the problem are so vast that the Economic and Social Council of the United Nations commissioned a special study in 1983. Roger Greenway, editor of *Urban Mission*, writes:

Prostitution can be found in varying degrees in all countries of the world, in all cultures, and especially in places where the population is dense, the poor are numerous and money flows freely...and it is in fact growing. For example, in one country where the three factors mentioned above are all found, the proportion of women between the ages of 15 and 30 living off prostitution is about 10 percent (March, 1984, page 17).

Prostitutes are sad victims of abuse. They live from day to day, beaten half to death by pimps, treated like cheap lovers, forced into dependency on drugs, exchanged for other prostitutes and even flown to foreign cities and countries to satisfy different customers. According to Greenway:

Through violence, threats and isolation from anyone that might help them, prostitutes are reduced to the point of having lost all self-esteem, even their personal identity. Their procurers [pimps] are their masters, and they are the slaves. Prostitution scars a woman's character so deeply, and creates such a gap between her and normal society, that few women ever manage to get out of it (page 19).

Prostitution is advanced by the 264 pornographic magazines published around the world, organized sex tours, military bases, topless bars and night clubs. It is big business, making a profit on human lust and the economic desperation of its victims. Most of those caught in the system enter prostitution because it's the only way they can put bread on the table. Young children are often forced into it by parents for this reason. In Paris alone, 8,000 boys and girls under the age of 18 work as prostitutes.

So sophisticated is this international exploitation, that prostitutes are *regularly* shipped from Southeast Asia to the Middle East, from Korea to North America and from France to Germany. Hardly any country is free from this international trafficking.

The Poverty Gap

Poverty runs like a common thread through the realities of urbanization, refugees and prostitution, but comparing the poorest and richest countries brings the issues of poverty into focus. The poorest third of the world's countries have average infant mortality rates of 140 deaths per 1,000 live births. Those who survive infancy can only expect to live to be 47; only 28 percent of the men and 9 percent of the women will ever learn to read. These countries have gross national products (GNP) averaging $320 per person per year.

Looking at the same statistics for the rich third of the

world's countries, it's hard to believe they share the same planet. Infant mortality rates are around 12 per 1,000 live births; average life expectancy is 74 years, literacy around 90 percent and GNP $18,405.

The cities, refugee camps, prostitution centers and poor areas are all places where the good news of the Kingdom needs to penetrate. But most of the people in these situations are hidden by yet another barrier—they identify with a non-Christian religion. There are spiritual as well as physical obstacles that the gospel faces in trying to reach them.

Spiritual Barriers

Islam is the largest non-Christian religion in the world today, claiming one out of every five people—850 million all together. Islam is on the rise in many areas, and, as a result, the Western stereotypes of Muslims are frequently tinged with fear.

But the stereotypes just can't fit the vast diversity of Muslim cultures, languages and lifestyles. Most Muslims aren't Arabs. Indonesia has more Muslims than any other country. Muslims can be found in major concentrations from the Straits of Gibraltar to the Great Wall of China. By the year 2,000, 35 percent of the Soviet Union will identify with Islam. Even in the West, 26 million Muslims live as students, refugees or businessmen.

Hinduism claims another 650 million followers, 90 percent of them in India. Worshiping a myriad of deities and placating all kinds of spirits, Hindus see themselves as locked into their karma or fate. Each is born into one of 3,000 distinct castes, from which he can never move. Apathy is a religious virtue.

Another 300 million are *Buddhists*. They believe

their lives are caught up in an endless cycle of reincarnation and suffering. Only the most religious can hope to attain a status known as nirvana. The rest are left to appeal to deities, fear evil spirits and earn merit by religious rituals.

Another 100 to 200 million people are part of tribal groups. Caught between the enduring strength of tribal relationships and the intrusions of the modern world, tribes are in flux around the world. Many tribes have accepted a veneer of Hinduism, Buddhism or Islam, but the vast majority are animists, bound to a variety of spirits. Five thousand distinct tribes still have no church.

We need one more key to put the picture together. Jesus' command tells us to "make disciples of all nations." Have all the nations been reached with his love?

The sun never sets on the Christian church—there are believers on every continent. Of the 223 countries, all but eight have strong Christian fellowships capable of healthy evangelism and deeds of mercy (although many of these fellowships are quite small).

What about the nations? "Wait a minute!" you might be saying, "Aren't nations the same as countries?"

The Nations Within Countries

Think for a moment about Kenya. Kenya was colonized by the British, who called the piece of property they claimed British East Africa. But prior to the British arrival, at least 24 different nations lived in that region—24 distinct tribes, each with its own language and ethnic identity. Those 24 nations still exist with the country of Kenya today.

The 24 tribes in Kenya are the "nations" to be discipled there. Kenya's population is 70 percent Christian, but half of the *nations* (or tribes) within the country have virtually no Christians. They have no churches, either, which are firmly enough established to be capable of bringing the good news to the rest of the people of that tribe.

All the continents have been reached. All but eight countries have been, as well. But *thousands* of nations remain unreached. These are the nations our generation has to focus on discipling in order to fulfill the great commission. The job won't be done until they have had the chance to hear the gospel in their own language and experience the joy of worshiping God within their own culture.

So who are these unreached peoples? Researchers estimate that there are at least 6,000 to 17,000 unreached peoples. World Vision International's mission research division, MARC, has fairly good descriptions of 3,500 of those peoples. Many more have been located, but have yet to be described. Most researchers agree that the total number of individuals in unreached peoples is around 2.5 billion—half the world's population. They are truly the hidden half—hidden from the light of the gospel, and hidden for the most part from the eyes of the church.

Where are the unreached people? By and large, they are found among those with the kind of needs we explored earlier. They are among the poor, in the exploding cities of the third world, in refugee camps. Most are part of one of the religions we mentioned. These charts help put the picture together.

The 20 Countries With
The Lowest Percentage of Christians

Country	Percent Christian	Primary Religion	Number of Identified and Described Unreached Peoples
1 Afghanistan	0.0	Islam	19
2 Nepal	0.0	Hinduism	37
3 North Yemen	0.0	Islam	4
4 Bhutan	0.1	Buddhism	4
5 Maldives	0.1	Islam	1
6 Somalia	0.1	Islam	1
7 Yemen	0.1	Islam	2
8 China	0.2	Chinese/ Islam	58
9 Mauritania	0.4	Islam	4
10 Niger	0.4	Islam	7
11 Oman	0.4	Islam	1
12 Turkey	0.5	Islam	8
13 Morocco	0.5	Islam	3
14 Bangladesh	0.5	Islam	11
15 Algeria	0.8	Islam	3
16 Saudi Arabia	0.8	Islam	2
17 Iran	0.9	Islam	45
18 Thailand	1.1	Buddhism/ Islam	35
19 Guinea	1.3	Islam	12
20 Libya	1.7	Islam	2

Major Religions

Religion	Number of People Millions	Ethnolinguistic Groups*
Islam	850	approx 4000
Hinduism	650	approx 3000
Buddhism	300	approx 1000
Tribalism	100	approx 3000
Chinese Traditionalism	200	approx 60

* Much research is still needed to refine the accuracy of these figures.

The 15 Countries With Lowest Gross National Product

Country	GNP ($U.S.)	Number of Identified and Described Unreached Peoples
1 Bhutan	80	4
2 Laos	80	16
3 Viet Nam	100	87
4 Chad	110	59
5 Ethiopia	140	70
6 Bangladesh	140	11
7 Nepal	150	37
8 Afghanistan	170	19
9 Guinea-Bissau	190	15
10 Mali	190	18
11 Burma	190	66
12 Malawi	200	8
13 Zaire	210	73
14 Burundi	230	2
15 Mozambique	230	15

21 of the 50 Largest Cities in the World are Populated Predominantly by Unreached Peoples

Number of Large Cities	Type of Unreached Peoples
8	Muslim
6	Chinese
4	Hindu
3	Buddhist

The 15 Countries With Highest Infant Mortality Rate (per 1,000 Live Births)

	Country	Rate	Number of Identified and Described Unreached Peoples
1	Upper Volta	210	33
2	Afghanistan	200	19
3	Sierra Leone	200	16
4	Yemen Arab Rep.	190	4
5	Malawi	170	8
6	Guinea	160	12
7	Angola	150	21
8	Benin	150	23
9	Bhutan	150	4
10	Cent. Afr. Rep.	150	27
11	Chad	150	59
12	Ethiopia	150	70
13	Guinea-Bissua	150	15
14	Liberia	150	18
15	Mali	150	18

Regions of the World
Unreached Peoples as Language Groups

Region	Total Languages	Number of Unreached Peoples*
Africa	1883	1034
East Asia	193	62
Europe	169	10
Latin America	1538	200
Northern America	250	11
Oceania	1253	629
South Asia	1596	976
USSR	128	59

* A total of 2,981 unreached peoples of different languages. The *total* number of unreached people groups is greater than this because many unreached peoples share languages.

A Special Effort

In an age where people wonder whether missionaries are relics from the past, the thousands of unreached peoples cry out for a flood of new missionaries.

If every Christian witnessed to every neighbor he could reach, that would still leave four-fifths of the non-Christians in the world without a chance to hear the good news. Those four-fifths are the unreached peoples—they have no Christian neighbors and no local church to tell them what it means to be a Christian. For them to hear, someone will have to cross the barriers of geography, language and culture to communicate the gospel in a way they can understand and respond to.

Discipling all the nations is a task for the whole church. It takes people who will seek out these hidden peoples—much like the master who prepared a banquet and ordered his slaves to search the highways and byways to find people who would come.

Making disciples of the unreached nations will take those with gifts of evangelism and church planting. The primary goal must be to establish churches in each of these groups which will live out the gospel in the cultural context of that people.

But the unreached are found among the world's neediest people, so making the Kingdom real to them will require missionary servants who will use just about every skill or vocation imaginable. The hungry must be fed, the sick healed, the outcasts given homes, the distraught comforted, the captives freed and the oppressed unburdened. It is the church, empowered by the Holy Spirit, that is God's primary instrument for announcing, embodying and effecting this sort of social transformation.

Jesus was thinking of the unreached peoples as he cleared the temple. The unreached peoples were invited into the inner sanctuary of the Holy of Holies when the curtain tore in two, and John saw peoples who are unreached today worshiping the King at his throne.

They're Waiting

Marilyn Laszlo is a missionary with Wycliffe Bible Translators. She told a story recently that summarizes the heart cry of the hidden half.

For the past thirteen years I have been working in Hauna, a little village which is 500 miles up the Sepik River in the heart of the jungle of Papua New Guinea, an island just north of Australia.

On the island of Papua New Guinea there are over 700 distinct languages, most of which are unwritten. Actually, there are over 3,000 language groups in the world that have no written language. They do not even have an alphabet, much less any books.

That is the way it was in Hauna Village, home of the Sepik Iwam people. They had no idea that the words that came out of their mouths could be written down.

My partner and I were given training in linguistics and we began learning the language one word at a time by pointing to objects and by acting out concepts. Eventually the Lord gave us a team of fourteen translation helpers to work with.

When we started translating, I became very burdened about the older people in the village. The witch doctors were being left out. They are the most powerful men in the village and are always busy because there is always someone sick or someone dying.

My partner and I wanted to have these older men come from 6:30 to 7:30 every night, after we had finished translating, and listen to the verses we had translated that day. So we had our translation helpers go out in teams of two to each of the four clans in the village and get one older man from each clan to join them.

Every day these witch doctors or "spitters" came to listen to the Word of God. Their word for doctor is *inkam hiiswoki*, which means "the man who spits" or "the spitter." If you have malaria the spitters take a sharp bamboo and cut your forehead where it hurts to let out the bad blood. Then they chew on a plant that supposedly contains a very powerful spirit, and they spit and blow into those cuts. This is the power that will help heal you.

We had translated a portion of the Gospel of Mark, chapter eight. As we were reading these verses we came to verse 23, the story of Jesus spitting on the eyes of the blind man to heal him. Now we have blind people in the village, but no medicine man has been able to heal them. So when we read this verse, the older men jumped up and said, "Wow! Why Jesus must be the most powerful spitter in the whole world!" From that day they started coming to church. They identified with this spitting man, Jesus, and wanted to know more about him.

As we translated and taught the people to read and write their own language, we became burdened for all of the unreached tribes around us. Hauna was becoming a shining light throughout the area as people started to hear about our work. One day a canoe loaded with fifteen people came for medical help. They spoke another tribal language and came into our house with the smell of their rotting sores and other diseases. I told them in the trade language, Pidgin English, that they must stay in our village at least a week so I could give them a penicillin series for their sores.

While they stayed with us they watched what was going on. They saw 200 people coming to school to learn to read and write their own language. They saw us write God's talk in the people's language and listened to the Sepik Iwam pastors preach the Word of God in their own language.

When it was time for them to go home, the leader asked, "Do you think you could come to my village and put down our talk so that we might know about God too?"

I had to shake my head and say, "I'm not finished here yet. I have several more years of work in this place." I could tell he was very disappointed, and I promised that someday I would at least come to visit his village.

Several weeks later we organized a party to find his village. When we got there, the leader was thrilled to see us. He called everybody to come and see the two white misses. As we were walking through the village I noticed in the center a new building, very different from their regular houses. I asked, "What is that building there in the center of the village?"

He said, "Oh, that is God's house—that's our church."

"Your church? Do you have a mission here?"

"Oh, no, we have never had a mission here."

"Well, do you have a pastor here—you know, someone that comes to preach God's Word?"

"Oh, no, we've never had a pastor here."

"Well, is there someone here in the village that can read and write Pidgin English who holds services in your church?"

"Oh, no! There is no one here that can read or write. And we have no books."

I looked at him and said, "Then what is that building for?"

He said, "Well, we saw the little church in your village and our people decided to build a church too. Now we're waiting for someone to come and tell us about God in our own talk."

I turned and started crying. I have never seen that kind of faith. Out in the middle of the jungle stands that little church, and today they are still waiting— waiting for someone to come and tell them in their own language about Jesus. There are thousands of groups just like them, waiting to hear the Word of God in their own language. They are waiting for you.

CHAPTER NINE

People on the Move

God's people *are* responding to these needs, and to his call to disciple all the nations.

David Barrett documents almost 250,000 missionaries at work worldwide. Granted, not all of them have understood the distinctive call to disciple all the nations, but they've understood enough of God's heart for the world to leave home, friends and comfort in order to take up life in another part of the globe to serve people in other cultures.

Of those 250,000 cross-cultural servants, 55,000 are Protestant missionaries sent from North America. Twenty years ago there were only 35,000 of them! The growth in the missionary force is just one encouraging sign that God is stirring up his people to a fresh understanding of his desire for the nations.

God's people are heading for the ends of the earth, creatively finding new ways to get the job done as they go along. Frontiers, a new mission agency, embodies this kind of faith, hope and love.

A Go-For-It Agency

We're starting from the premise that we shouldn't go from our experience, but from the declared intentions of God—the fact that he will build his church. When we look at the Muslim world and see it's not happening, our conclusion is that it is due to happen.

This, as founder and director Greg Livingstone expresses it, is Frontiers' operating assumption. As a young mission, Frontiers has the ambitious goal of putting 2,000 new missionaries on the field in 200 Muslim people groups by the year 2000. Bold faith and innovative strategies are only the beginning of what's new in Frontiers' approach.

Livingstone himself is a fireball with a talent for motivating others to believe God for great things. He tells the story of how he first became aware of the Muslim world as a Wheaton College student in 1959.

> I was invited to an all-night prayer meeting, and more out of pride than anything else, I went to see what in the world is an all-night prayer meeting. I walked in the room and George Verwer said, "What country are you claiming, brother?"
>
> I asked, "What's left?"
>
> And he said, "Libya, you got Libya."
>
> We spent the whole night hovering over maps of Libya and Turkey and Afghanistan and Indonesia, and praying that God would send laborers to these places. God impressed on me that night that my ambitions were too small. I could get in on what he was doing in the world.
>
> I know that my eyes are open to the needs of the Muslims, and other people's aren't—people who are just as spiritual as me or even more so. I don't scold people for not having a burden for Muslims. That's God's problem. I'm a lot less judgmental than I was. All I know is he opened my eyes, and I'm supposed to do something about it, and I'm going to find 2,000 other people to do something about it.

Livingstone's vision of God's love for Muslims continued to grow during his 14 years as a leader with Operation Mobilization, a new agency that his friend George Verwer founded to get young people involved with the needs of people around the world. Later he joined North Africa Mission (NAM), and served as the U.S. Director.

Working with NAM, Greg became convinced that if Muslims were to have the opportunity to hear, many more missionaries would need to go to them. He began to see that traditional means of recruiting, training and sending missionaries weren't enough. He started a new "rapid deployment" branch of NAM (known as NAM Associates) to send teams to the Arab countries where missionaries are outnumbered by Muslims a million to one. In June, 1983, NAM Associates became Frontiers, an independent "daughter" spinoff of NAM.

Frontiers' decision to merge with the Maldive Islands Outreach effectively opened up the entire Muslim world to the new agency. In its first 15 months, Frontiers has grown to almost 200 coworkers. By the end of 1984, they expect to have over 90 missionaries on the field in 16 teams, from London to Morocco to the Arab Gulf to China and Indonesia. Another hundred are preparing to go.

How have they managed to put so many people on some of the toughest mission fields in the world so quickly? "We're convinced that we're involved in a movement of God," says David Mowen, Director of Training.

The new mission has some effective recruiters including Livingstone, who is a well-known speaker, and Bob Sjogren, a young enthusiast who regularly travels to college campuses sharing his experiences in Libya and other Muslim countries and challenging students with the vision of Frontiers. But more and more, says Mowen, people are coming to Frontiers saying, "The Lord has given me a burden for Saudi Arabia, can you help me get there?"

As Mowen explains, "If it's a movement of God, there's little we can do to control it." Where other missions decide which field they will work in, plan strategies, and recruit people for the necessary positions, Frontiers tends to act as a facilitator for people who sense God's guidance to a particular part of the world. A new field is opened up as soon as someone shows up who is qualified to lead a team of six to twelve missionaries. Then the team leader and headquarters staff recruit the rest of the team, design a creative way to get into the country, come up with a strategy and set goals.

Various teams have found creative strategies for getting into Muslim countries. Frontiers' members work at anything from teaching English to developing hydroponics (water-based agriculture) projects, to starting new business enterprises. It's hard to describe a typical team or typical members.

Frontiers' teams are composed of people in three basic roles. First is the leader, an "apostle" with gifts and leadership skills to direct a church-planting effort. Team leaders aren't always experienced missionaries. Currently Frontiers teams are led by such people as a former youth pastor, an IBM salesman, and an ex-Marine sergeant.

The second part of the team is composed of disciple-makers: people who enjoy working with others and building them up in their relationships with Jesus.

The third part of the team are those who play supportive roles, having secular skills that give the team a reason for being in the country or contributing practical skills to the team. People with all kinds of educational and vocational backgrounds are finding places on Frontiers teams.

Commitment to reaching Muslims and willingness to believe God for the "impossible" are the unifying characteristics of the agency. As Mowen explains, "People said it was impossible to get more than a 72-hour pass into the Arab Gulf, but our people there now have two-year visas."

Greg puts it more starkly. He's sending out people who want to do more than just survive in "closed" countries. "In the past, people have gone out with the mentality, 'I mustn't get kicked out, so what can I do so I don't get kicked out?' They're already backpedaling." He encourages an attitude that would say, "of course" to any question. "We believe we can build respect by being right up front—culturally sensitive so we don't make them defiant or defensive—but matter of fact about why we're there"—even if it means getting into trouble with the government!

Livingstone takes his cue from Acts 4—Peter and John's refusal to stop speaking in the name of Jesus.

That's the message we have from the whole Muslim world—stop speaking in the name of Jesus. We have to come back with the same reaction as Peter and John: "We cannot help speaking about the things we have seen and heard." Just because we get a letter that says leave, *where* do we have the biblical basis to say we're supposed to leave? Where is anybody saying, "Excuse me, I'm not leaving because God told me to come, and he hasn't told me to leave?"

Greg suggests this attitude may mean prison for some of his missionaries. "That's a normal New Testament experience. It's the American church that's abnormal!"

Livingstone is convinced that, confronted with a strong stand for Christ, Muslims are going to turn to the Lord. "If it's only going to prison and refusing to leave that will get them to believe we're serious about our faith, then we'll have to be ready to pay that price."

Every Tongue

Another dynamic group sprang up earlier in this century. This year they are celebrating their 50th anniversary, and Wycliffe Bible Translators have a lot to be thankful for.

A Mexican Indian once challenged founder Cameron Townsend: "If your God is so great, why doesn't he speak my language?"

Cam took the challenge and organized Wycliffe with the goal of putting the Bible into every language on earth. He recognized translation as a key part of advancing God's desire to see every people reached with his love.

Wycliffe now has more than 5,000 staff (approximately 3,750 from North America). They completed their 200th New Testament translation last year, and at least portions of the Bible now exist in 1,763 languages. That covers 97 percent of the world's population. (It still needs to get into all those people's hands!) The remaining 3 percent of the world speaks 3,000 different languages. Wycliffe has no plans for retreat. Their hope is to add another 3,000 missionaries in the next decade.

The Young Rise to the Call

Twenty-five years ago a young man in his early twenties had a vision of young people going out to all the world as waves crashing against the shore. He couldn't shake this vivid picture and so eventually stepped out in faith to begin Youth With a Mission (YWAM).

Today Loren Cunningham is still leading that group of youth, and God has given him more than 5,000 full-time cross-cultural servants. In addition, 10,000 to 15,000 others participate in six-month programs every year.

YWAM has had as its goal to penetrate all 223 countries in the world with the love of Jesus. They've nearly reached it, and Loren told me recently that YWAM's next goal is to reach *all the nations*, to go to the unreached peoples of the world!

Yes, God is definitely spurring his church on to action, to faith-filled, hope-based, love-driven ministry aimed at nothing short of discipling all the nations.

Language Institute for Evangelism (LIFE), aimed primarily at Japan, and International Students Inc. (ISI), aimed primarily at internationals in the United States, are two other organizations with great ministries and great promise, whose lifeblood is in youth.

Other young groups are on the move.

A few college students from Pennsylvania State University went to one of the most anti-Christian countries in the world for a year, just to demonstrate that God's heart for the nations couldn't be stopped by anything. Then they founded *Caleb Project*. Headed up by Greg Fritz (in his twenties), Caleb project hopes to influence 100,000 people to become missionaries to nations that are yet unreached. Their basic goal is to help Christians mature in their commitment to reach the nations. Only 5 years old, they already have "Calebites" on more than 100 campuses. A similar group has sprung up in Australia as well.

Another student group, *Theological Students For Frontier Missions* (TSFM), is going full steam under the leadership of a Princeton graduate, Bill Campbell.

Bill believes that if seminaries get their focus on discipling all the nations, then churches will be radically affected. Besides influencing the U.S. seminaries, Bill has been hard at work in helping seminarians in India, Korea, Hong Kong and Singapore.

Inter-Varsity Missions operates at full tilt motivating and educating students. John Kyle and David Bryant write books, produce videos, hold training camps and conferences, and run short-term mission projects. The famous URBANA missions convention draws up to 17,000 participants every three years. In both 1979 and 1981, 10,000 students stood to announce their intention to make their lives count for the sake of the unreached.

Kyle, a Wycliffe missionary on loan to Inter-Varsity, is very clear in his goals for all of his frantic activity: "If I wasn't convinced that all of this stuff was going to result in laborers to the unreached, I'd give it all up and head back for the mission field."

His partner, David Bryant, has recently given leadership to a burgeoning movement called "Concerts of Prayer." The program of these concerts is *prayer*—prayer for revival and world evangelization.

Hundreds of churches and organizations are joining in.

"Perspectives on the World Christian Movement" is an accredited course designed to teach a clear understanding of the biblical call to reach all the nations. Designed principally by two young adults, Jay Gary and Steve Hawthorne, this course is now taken by over 1,000 students every year in extension programs around the country.

Publications

Getting information about the world in the hands of God's people is a key part of mobilizing a new missions thrust. Several important publications have appeared in the past few years.

Started by two college students and now staffed by 30 people mostly in their twenties and early thirties, WORLD CHRISTIAN Magazine reaches young adults who have a view of life that says, "Going all out to reach all the nations." Less than 3 years old, this bi-monthly, four-color magazine is read regularly by 45,000 activists.

The Global Prayer Digest, a daily devotional guide focused on the unreached peoples, is published by the Frontier Fellowship, a national organization devoted to getting Christians involved in prayer and giving for the frontiers.

Missions Advanced Research and Communications Center (MARC, a division of World Vision) has been publishing the annual *Unreached Peoples* series since 1979. Each issue lists several thousand groups yet unpenetrated with the gospel. MARC also publishes a newsletter, materials on how to strategize to penetrate an unreached people group and unreached people prayer cards to assist people in intercession.

In 1983, David Barrett released the gigantic *World Christian Encyclopedia.* This massive volume analyzes Christian and non-Christian populations in every country, and has already become an invaluable tool for mission strategists.

Organizations of the Older Crew

Older organizations haven't been standing still. Over 400 Protestant mission agencies founded by previous generations to bring the gospel where it has not yet gone, are nurturing the ministries they birthed in new cultures while at the same time setting their sights on unreached groups. They have a rich history of sacrifice and servanthood for the sake of those outside the Kingdom.

In 1974, Billy Graham called together 4,000 leaders with the message, "We are responsible for the evangelization of this whole generation of the whole world." Out of that meeting in Lausanne, Switzerland, came the Lausanne Committee for World Evangelization (LCWE), a loose network serving thousands of mission leaders worldwide. The committee has initiated hundreds of consultations to equip the church to reach the unreached and has published dozens of papers outlining the srategies needed to win specific peoples. The LCWE also sponsors seminars and workshops that help pastors in their local settings to recognize and make plans to reach the peoples right around them.

In 1976, Dr. Ralph D. Winter founded the U.S. Center for World Mission (USCWM) on a college campus in Pasadena, California, as a base for educating the

North American church on the needs of the un-reached. This center, although the campus is not yet paid for, has brought 60 organizations together to cooperate in the common goal of discipling the nations. Associated with the USCWM, William Carey International University offers graduate and under-graduate programs to equip Christians for the work of discipling the unreached.

The list of people and initiatives dedicated to dis-cipling all the nations goes on, and that's good news! Many Christians are waking up in a fresh manner to what God is doing, and they want to be a part of it.

Warmed-Over-Jonah

The book of Acts shows the amazing things that band of twelve disciples did when they had fully grasp-ed the love story of the Bible. But that kind of faith-filled living was never meant for just apostles or a few radicals. The privilege and responsibility of discipling the nations belongs to the whole church.

Activists are popping up all over, yet the church as a whole has yet to wake up and join in. Many Christians still reflect the attitude of our friend Jonah. The average annual giving of each North American Chris-tian to overseas missions last year was *less than $15*. The combined assets of the churches of one small California city are greater than the *total annual* giving of the whole North American church to overseas mis-sions. Sounds like Jonah warmed over.

Our church has not only failed to spend its resour-ces reaching out to the nations—but it even rejects the nations when Jesus brings them to its door. Don Bjork of World Relief says that the U.S. church has retreated in its willingness to help refugees and immigrants.

We're worried about our rights and security rather than about the awful suffering of these poor, displaced people. And the Scriptures demand that we take them in. The small, less-developed country of Pakistan took in more refugees during 1978 and 1979 than the United States has since 1945.

All the nations will be reached. God has promised it, and God is faithful to his promises. Already thousands of Christians are discovering the joy of finding their role in this great venture.

The question is: will your life and mine count in this global love story? Will we allow God to saturate us with his love, faith and hope so he will be able to work *through* us to bring all the nations to himself? That's what the rest of the book is about—how to refuse to be a warmed-over-Jonah.

CHAPTER TEN

The Problem of the Big Chill

Not too long ago, I was invited to speak at the missions emphasis week at my old college. I was supposed to tell the young excitables there what a "world Christian" is.

Quite pleased to have the chance to affect another set of college students, I stepped up to the podium. I looked out on a crowd of new faces, but the scene felt very familiar. I had stood there many times as a student, urging my peers to commit themselves all-out to Jesus Christ and his global mission. And from the audience, I had listened to a number of fellow students challenge the student body to the same vision.

But, as I stood there thinking about the "campus radicals" of my college days, all my good memories melted away. I felt as if someone had hit me with a ton of bricks.

Where were those radicals now? A good percentage had slipped into a way of life that showed no more passion or activism than selling used cars. The vision that seemed to capture their very lives during their college years had vanished like a mist. Their passion had no substance; their convictions turned out to be shadows.

That night I came to a new understanding of what it means to be a world Christian. It had to be more than words, more than a few years of activism. My commitment has real substance only if I can't separate my passion for the world from my identity as a person. Being a world Christian is first and foremost who I am, not just what I say or do.

Students tend to be susceptible to visions of changing the world. Just look at the radicals of the 1960's. They were out to change a lot of things in the world around them, and some even died for their convictions. They staged riots, denounced abusive capitalism, burned banks, opposed trade with oppressive regimes and called for an end to war—all in the name of making the world a better place.

What happened to those radicals? A popular movie, "The Big Chill," gives a glimpse of where some of them ended up a few years later. They became managers, stock brokers, up-the-ladder career climbers, movie stars and big landowners. They bought into everything they used to stand against. The characters in the movie obviously felt uncomfortable about the disjointedness of their past radicalism and their present lifestyles. They couldn't figure out what went wrong with their great plans to change the world.

I'm sure none of us would imagine ourselves letting go of our commitments to see all nations reached. None of my college peers thought they would, either, but somehow the pressures they faced after college proved too much for them.

Finding Zeal

To understand some of these pressures, let's look at the typical pattern of development in our culture during and after college years. First, most of us go from *dependence* to *independence* as we enter college.

Up to this point, our parents have been responsible

for us—they even reported us on their tax forms as "dependents." They took care of rent, food, clothes, activities. They made major decisions for us or had a big part in helping us make them. Without realizing it, we absorbed many of their political and religious views.

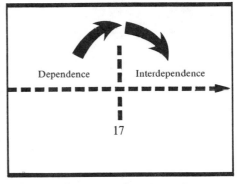

Around the age of seventeen things begin to change. If I go to college, I am surrounded by a whole new set of people. Maybe for the first time I discover that Baptists also consider themselves Christians, or I meet charismatics that seem to love Jesus more than I do.

New ideas come at me a mile a minute. Perhaps I take a class in anthropology that harshly berates Western Christians for going to other parts of the world and "ruining cultures." Or I take a class in apologetics or philosophy, and instead of understanding my beliefs more clearly, I find my foundations shaken. Maybe I meet some Marxists who have a better handle on understanding how society works than I do, and so I begin to doubt my own political orientation. I may find a job and begin to pay my own expenses and make decisions about my life that others used to make for me.

This process of shaking up old ideas and beliefs and being exposed to new ones in an environment of independence makes people at this stage more idealistic than they ever will be again.

No wonder the first time I plunge into an urban center I want to do all I can to help the displaced; or the first time I see actual starvation I decide to drastically reduce my eating habits and watch my spending; or the first time it hits me that half the world still does not know Jesus I decide to become a missionary!

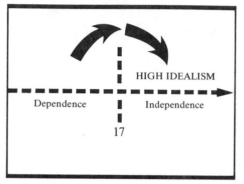

HIGH IDEALISM

Dependence   Independence

17

All these could be called *reactions* that challenge our previous actions. We throw out old values and decide to live our lives differently. Like the radicals of the 1960's, more than likely we have a clearer picture of what we are against than what we are for. Many of us during this time of life could be described as angry people. Angry at our homes, angry at our friends, angry at our churches, angry at our schools, angry at our nation.

Even if this reaction doesn't come out as anger, there is a high level of excitement and energy. It's during this stage of idealism that most of us stand at missions conventions. "Yes! We will do it!" we announce. Our sincere hearts are wide open before God as he shows us his passion for the nations. We can't do anything but say, "Yes, Lord, use me." And it shouldn't be any other way!

Idealism's great rush to put new ideas and convictions into practice is good, but it's only the beginning. It's easy to eat less and cut expenses when you're surrounded by others committed to simple lifestyle. The idealist too often fails to look at his commitment as the start of a lifelong venture. College days and idealism don't last forever. How can the values and behaviors explored there become enough a part of me to stick when I'm taken out of a supportive, or at least tolerant, environment?

Adding Knowledge

Proverbs 19:2 instructs: "It is not good to have zeal without knowledge, or to be hasty and miss the way." The key to the next major transition is knowledge—a firm biblical understanding that will sustain us over the long haul.

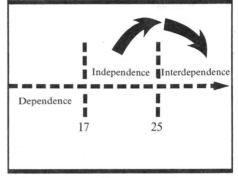

Not long after graduation, usually around 25 years of age, I begin to discover that I don't live in complete independence. In reality I am *interdependent* with other people and with institutions in our society. If I don't do a good job at work, I don't get a raise or I get fired. I buy a car or a house, but now I'm committed to the bank and my payment schedule. If I get married I discover that all my decisions, dreams and plans are now intimately connected to someone else. And the arrival of children makes that interdependence all the more inescapable.

If independence is a time of high idealism, then the beginning of interdependence is just the opposite. It feels like a wet blanket or a slap in the face. It's during this stretch of life that we will throw away our ideas if they were shallow, if they had no real substance.

These first few years of interdependence force us to determine how we will live out our ideals. We either put them in the crucible of new pressures and responsibilities to refine and *strengthen* our vision, or we decide they don't fit with reality and we just put our plans for changing the world on ice. I call this early stage of interdependence "Big Chill country."

Making it Through "Big Chill Country"

In Big Chill country you realize in no uncertain terms that the goals of the culture around you (which you find making increasing demands on you as you become interdependent) and God's goal of reaching the nations with his love have little to do with each

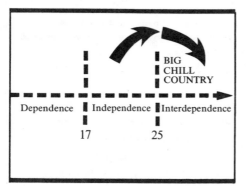

other. You're going to have a tough time fulfilling your culture's expectation while you try to stay faithful to your vision for the nations. Here's where you have to decide whose side you're really on. Everyone around you— from your boss to your church to your family—will probably do their best to put the chill on your determination to make your life count for the nations. And it's going to seem a lot easier just to become another Jonah.

If your ideas were based on shallow grounding, there will be nothing but personal grits available to help you stick to the vision. But if you have sunk your roots deep down into Jesus and his approach to life, you will have all the resources of heaven backing you up as you move forward.

Some of us, like my friend Cath in chapter two, hit Big Chill country and run away to the mountains because we just can't put it all together. Others just drop the vision and try to blend into society. But some, by God's grace, are described by their friends years later as people who faithfully lived out the ideals of their youth, those who integrated a biblical view of reality into their whole lives.

"Sit down young man! If God wants to evangelize the heathen he'll do it without your help or mine." That was the reaction William Carey got from the elders of his church when he suggested sending missionaries to the millions of unreached peoples of his day. The church in his generation didn't have any categories for such a venture—it didn't fit into their notions of

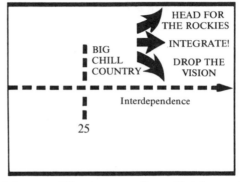

what the church was all about. They weren't excited about some young radical telling them what to do either.

But Carey wasn't about to be discouraged. He kept praying, accumulating information on the needs of the world, and studying God's heart for the world in Scripture. Carey's convictions became so much a part of him that there was no keeping him home, try as everyone around him might.

Carey is known today as the father of Protestant missions from the English-speaking world. It was said of him that his life was basically the outworking of the dreams of his youth. He went through Big Chill country, but his basis was firm.

What are We Up Against?

Let's take a close look at some of the dynamics.

You rush home all excited about your newfound vision to reach the world with Jesus' love. Your folks tell you they're happy for you, but explain that you'll eventually realize that all good Christians are supposed to "grow up, settle down, get a secure, well-paying job and be a good Christian." *Drop the temperature a few degrees.*

Say your parents *paid* for your education. Guilt settles in as they tell you just how much they sacrificed to ensure you could lead a responsible life and take care of them as they got older. And besides, you're the one, of all the children in the family, that they were really counting on, because you "had things going for you." *I think I feel a draft!*

Maybe you get married and your spouse has a different view of the good life. You made the mistake of marrying someone who wasn't committed to your ideals. Or maybe you are committed to the same ideals, but have children. Your parents become outraged that you are considering overseas service and they lay it on thick that no loving God would expect poor, helpless little children to be thrust into those awful conditions. Think about your *children*, not yourselves! *B-b-b-brrrrr!*

Let's say you get a good job. All of a sudden the things you condemned in your idealistic days are actually within your grasp. You used to decry money being spent on fancy cars, big houses, exotic restaurants, expensive vacations and all sorts of technological gadgets, but now you have the power to own them! Maybe you'll splurge and then realize that there was nothing in it and let go. Maybe you'll begin to enjoy living with a few luxuries, and convince yourself that you really "need" them. *It's getting downright chilly!*

Anthropologists have done us a big favor in this area. They explain that at our core is a basic view of reality—a worldview. That worldview determines who we are, what we will value, and how we behave.

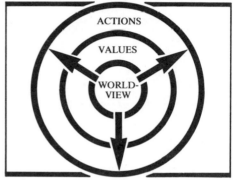

If our worldview is un-Christian or less-than-biblical, it will inevitably surface in values and actions that contradict the heart of the biblical worldview. And this is where the conflict arises during the Big Chill. If it turns out that I haven't really changed my worldview while I was idealistically exploring new values and actions, then I will give up my ideals and take on the culture's lifestyle. This is precisely what Solomon was saying in Proverbs 19:2; if we don't get something solid under our zeal, we're sure to miss the way.

But if my actions stem from a biblical worldview, then it becomes a matter of *faithful obedience.* I can allow a fad to slip away, but not something that goes as deep as obedience. I've decided to follow Jesus with my whole life, and I understand where he's going. It's no longer a matter of choosing a career or lifestyle—it's a matter of faithfulness.

Let's take a look at the biblical worldview Jonah needed.

CHAPTER ELEVEN

On Being "Sold Out"

Jonah's first problem was that he bought into his culture's worldview. He didn't see people the way God did, and so he couldn't figure out why God would show mercy on Ninevah.

A Christian worldview starts with God, not with country or church. God loves a Muslim as much as he does Billy Graham. We have to let go of prejudices and fears and see *all* people as precious. Our country isn't more valuable in God's eyes than any other, nor can the privileges it offers be more valuable in our eyes than living out God's mission.

A world Christian isn't a revolutionary out to tear down the government, but he is able to look beyond his national loyalty and say, "I have to love the world more than I love my country. " And he even has to go a step further, "I love the world more than I love my life."

A Matter of Obedience

Jonah didn't understand God's global heart. But that is only one-half of his worldview problem. Once God told Jonah what to do, he went the other way—he refused to obey. The biblical Christian worldview doesn't leave room for a life oriented to anything other than fulfilling our Lord's desires. What our God wants and what we do are inseparable items.

This is hard on North American Christians. We

have grown up in a society that tells us we are in charge of our own lives. We decide how they should unfold. We have the right to decide where we will be ten years from now. Our church even tells us that we have the right to decide whether God's desire for the nations will be a priority in our lives!

Any cultural worldview that places me, the individual, at the center of my life is 100 percent *anti-Christian*. God alone has the right to be at the center.

For Sale!

Imagine with me for a moment what it must have been like to be a slave in the New Testament days. If your master decides to sell you, you are taken to the marketplace in downtown Jerusalem and lined up with all the other items marked "for sale."

A prospective buyer comes along, examines your teeth, hands and biceps and decides to purchase you. The money exchanges hands and you are now the property of a new master.

Your master's day of shopping over, he loads you into the donkey cart with all his other acquisitions and takes you home. Once there, he takes you around the back to a little dwelling, and shows you where you sleep, what utensils you have for eating and the clothing he has provided for you.

Then he takes you around to the tool shed and points out the tools you are to use in the fields. All of these are provided—from food to tools—to equip you to make the master's plans happen. You don't wake up in the morning and wonder whether you feel like obeying your master that day—it just isn't an option for you.

Do you get the picture? Paul writes in I Corinthians 6:19-20 that we do not belong to ourselves, that we are slaves, bought at a price. The New Testament Christians knew just what Paul meant by this. They had seen the slaves for sale at the market every day, and some even had slaves at work in their own homes.

Obviously our Lord never does anything to us that is not for our good, and he never treats us with anything but love. But just as he is our loving Father and we are subjects of the heavenly King, so he is also our Master, and we are his slaves.

Jonah didn't view himself that way—he thought he could decide not to obey. Much of *our* cultural Christianity is Jonah warmed over when it sets up our plans and agendas apart from the ones God has revealed.

Let's Get Specific

Remember the diagram with worldview at the center, values next, and actions on the outside? Let's see what obeying this biblical worldview of God's heart for the nations looks like in contrast to the values and actions our culture promotes.

Where do we derive our identity?

The message of our culture is "be somebody," "get status," "look out for number one." These values go deep in our country—we're a nation of individualists, each trying somehow to stand out above the crowd. We spend our lives striving for the possessions and positions that will make us feel significant.

Does a slave try to "be somebody?" No, his whole existence is wrapped up in the master's identity. He's just an extension of what the master is all about. Jim Elliot, one of five missionaries martyred in Ecuador in the 1950's, once said, "We're just a bunch of nobodies trying to exalt Somebody." The only true identity a Christian has is in Christ—being a child of the King.

With his identity and personal worth wrapped up in Christ, the Christian is freed from the need to "be somebody." He can pour the money he would have spent on status symbols into discipling the nations. He can even pass up a promotion if it would lure him away from work that will advance what is on the Lord's heart.

What do we live for?

It's the "American Dream." Be free, be in charge, have lots of money, surround yourself with "good" things, put distance between yourself and the needy. As a culture, we pursue it with passion.

This dream is nonsense to a slave of Jesus Christ. How can a slave throw all his energy into building his own kingdom, when he's working full-time on his master's? And worse than nonsense, the American dream is completely self-centered and unloving in the light of God's global dream.

We've got to ask ourselves from time to time if we have any passion in life that is greater than our passion to see all the nations fall in love with Jesus. As Jesus cried, "It is finished," and the temple curtain tore in two, we saw his passion. He had endured the agony, pain and persecution so that the nations might enter into his life. His next job was to return to the heavens and prepare a place at the banquet table for all of those we invite as we continue to live out *his* passion.

Where are we going?

More than our identity and motivation, the biblical worldview challenges our plans. Our culture loves to talk about careers—from an early age we're encouraged to plot out our career paths right to the chairman of the board. We weigh decisions carefully, seeking the option that will serve our future best.

If our identity is truly found in Christ, then our vocational plans will be subject to what Jesus is doing in the world. The slave has no right to do anything but what the master tells him to do. He is acutely aware that all his time belongs to his master.

How do we use our resources?

Our American church has often communicated the view that we give God ten percent of our money (excluding all of our other material goods) and then the other 90 percent is for our "personal" use. In fact, the offering is often received in church services with a prayer to the effect that we are "giving back to you a portion of what you've given us."

Imagine the slave telling the master that he was going to give back a portion of the tools to him! Absurd. The idea of tithing in the Old Testament was simply instructions on how a *specific* ten percent was to be spent. The rest was still the Lord's. Israel was blessed to be a blessing. They were to use their resources for the sake of the nations.

The Christian who has truly caught hold of the passion of God's heart doesn't worry about which is his part and which is God's. He is so in love with Jesus that he can't think of anything but making every bit of his life count for the Kingdom—houses, cars, gadgets, salaries—all of it! And he will search out the areas of greatest need.

Preparing for Battle!

Remember the "Big Chill Country"? It's where we decide which worldview—our culture's or the

Bible's—will guide our values and actions during our adult years. The battle rages. It can temper our convictions or it can leave us with our ideals packed up and shoved in the deep freeze as a remnant of our youth.

Many mistakes are made during the heat of this exchange, poor decisions made and a lot of "garbage" added to the asset list. But victory comes as we determine to put our lives and lot fully with the Lord and his global desires. We are freed up as we admit mistakes, reverse bad decisions, and release superfluous pursuits and possessions in order to take hold of the things at God's heart.

Most of my friends who lost their vision lost it in Big Chill Country. And those who are really making their lives count for the nations went through this cultural battle, and emerged with a biblical worldview deeply integrated into the very core of who they are.

It shouldn't be strange in light of this to realize that the fastest growing churches in the world are those that have gone through the fire of persecution. Having searched their hearts to decide whether their lives would be fully identified with Christ and his commands, no matter what the cost, those Christians face the world with the love of Jesus in a way that just won't quit.

For those of us who live in comfort and can't even imagine persecution, the battle is more subtle. But it's just as important to decide.

Let's make sure our worldview is biblically based. Go for broke studying the Word to firmly plant in your heart his desire to see all the nations come to him. And then practice faithful obedience to him at every turn. Don't even *think* of saying "no" to your Lord. A small trickle of resistance quickly turns into a waterfall of rebellion. Follow the Master's will at all costs, and your life will begin to take on the stamp of faith, hope and love.

We don't have the capacity within ourselves to make our lives count for the nations. When we stop trying to make our plans happen and stop pursuing our personal interests, we become free to let God cause us to live in true abundance, free to let God live his life *through* us. A world Christian, because he lives committed to the worldview that flows from the heart of Jesus, is set free to pour his whole life into that world and watch Christ's love take effect.

Explore

Now that we understand some of the challenges ahead as we seek to integrate God's worldview into our lives, we can explore some areas of service. We know that God will use our lives to bring the nations to him, and we're willing to let him call the shots on the specific ways he wants to use us.

The issue is not, "be a missionary," but rather "pour your whole life into this mission venture." Obviously there are far too few missionaries, and God will guide thousands and thousands more into cross-cultural ministry. But I'm confident that if we have securely latched on to this biblical worldview, we'll discover that the issue of guidance is a small thing. Once I've hooked up with God's mission, God will plug me into the appropriate role.

Be sure that you don't become too fixed on finding "just the right" vocation. In his sovereignty, God may guide you through several vocational paths. He may be leading you to some role that you aren't even aware of today.

The next two chapters are designed to give you specific help in understanding two major arenas in which God moves to reach the nations. The first is the cross-cultural—"missions." The second I have called "counter-cultural," which involves living out the biblical worldview in the local church arena.

CHAPTER TWELVE

Cross-Cultural Servants

How often have you heard the saying, "Every Christian should be a missionary right where they are?" The idea that comes across is that being a missionary means simply "telling others about Jesus."

I suspect that most people who call us to this sort of task are sincere in their desire to see all Christians be thoroughly committed to Jesus Christ and actively involved in witnessing to those around them. Unfortunately, the word "missionary" loses its very meaning in this kind of appeal.

A missionary is someone who crosses cultural barriers to reach people who otherwise would not have an opportunity to hear about God's love. Paul wrote, "How can they believe in the one of whom they have not heard? And how can they hear without someone preaching to them? And how can they preach *unless they are sent?*" (Romans 10:14-15). Missionaries are *sent.* The world is desperately in need of *missionaries.*

What Should Today's Missionary Look Like?

One thing is certain—don't bother packing your pith helmet!

Wild stories of people fighting off snakes with machetes and eating cockroaches as the main course still can be found, but they are definitely in the minority.   The majority of today's and tomorrow's missionaries will be living in urban centers. They will be riding in buses and taxis, eating beans, rice and other cheap staples, and wearing western-looking clothes.

The new missionary needs to know about world events and trends. The globe is shrinking so fast that even remote areas aren't isolated. In many areas, the way people receive Westerners is affected by what they hear in the popular media.

Today's missionary has the privilege of being a servant in a way that missionaries of an earlier generation didn't. By identifying with those he serves, the missionary can break down some of the stereotypes third world people have about the West. People in the third world are used to Western businesses and countries ignoring their needs and exploiting their resources; a Westerner coming to them as a servant would attract their attention. Very often new missionaries will work under the leadership of Christians from the host country—another reversal of the usual third world pattern.

Modern missions also means a place for *almost any talents!* Missionaries serve as church planters and computer programmers, teachers and technicians, evangelists and engineers.

No matter what your role or skills, being a missionary means being a *servant.* In the secular market I approach companies with my skills and barter with them.   How much money and what sort of other benefits can I expect to get in exchange for 40 hours of labor? When I'm looking for a place to serve as a missionary, I'm not looking for a great job opportunity that will use every skill I have or advance my career. I'm looking for a way to advance the Kingdom.

Channels for Service

Mission agencies are channels that God uses to help Christians have an effective ministry on the field. Various kinds of agencies have evolved in the past 200 years—let's take a quick look at where they came from.

Not long after the elders told William Carey to be quiet, he published a little book with an enormous title: *An Enquiry Into the Obligation of Christians to Use Means for the Conversion of the Heathen.*

It wouldn't make the bestseller list today, but it galvanized the church in England to get involved in God's mission. Carey argued that Western Christians had to organize themselves, or form agencies, to reach those without the gospel around the world. The first mission agency from the English-speaking world sent Carey to India in 1793, and over the next few decades, a dozen other societies were born in England and America as a result of Carey's vision.

These first mission agencies were almost all tied to denominations. They focused on reaching the coastal areas of Africa and Asia, establishing a foothold in largely uncharted lands at the cost of hundreds of missionary lives.

For the next major mission thrust, God raised up a new mission structure. Hudson Taylor had a growing burden for China's 400 million people—especially those out of reach of the missionaries stationed along the coast. He founded the China Inland Mission in 1865, believing God would supply the people and funds. It was the first "faith mission"—drawing personnel from many denominations and supported by gifts from individuals and churches.

Soon many other new agencies burst into being, all

committed to reaching into the interiors of Asia and Africa. Their names embodied their goals—Sudan Interior Mission, Africa Inland Mission, Regions Beyond Missionary Union.

The twentieth century forever changed the landscape of missions. Two world wars, and the West lost its colonies. Technological advances multiplied geometrically. Evangelicals became aware once again that the gospel speaks to the needs of the whole person. The vast numbers of unreached peoples slowly came into view of mission strategists. Again, new structures arose to help people do the job God was calling them to.

Many of the agencies formed since 1945 focus on specialized tasks—Wycliffe Bible Translators work only with tribes that lack scriptures in their language or the ability to read them. Missionary Aviation Fellowship serves other agencies by flying missionaries and equipment into remote areas. Far East Broadcasting Company and Trans World Radio take advantage of radio technology to reach into "closed" countries.

In addition, a number of agencies have sprung up in the past 25 years that can probably be best described as non-traditional. They focus on mobilizing and training young people through short-term, team-based exposures to cross-cultural ministry. Operation Mobilization and Youth With a Mission are the largest of these agencies. While just a few years ago it was unheard of to let "inexperienced kids" loose on the mission field, today thousands of young people get their first exposure to the needs of the world through short term missions. Many come home determined to go back long term.

Getting on Board

Missionaries and agencies are partners. The missionary comes to serve the agency—to help it accomplish the task God has put on the hearts of the agency and the individual. The agency in turn nurtures the missionary, offering training, advice, guidance, structure to help him grow in his ministry.

Choosing a mission board means linking up with a group of people with whom you can be an effective partner. Each board has its distinctives—denominational ties, training requirements or programs, doctrinal preferences, means of support, size and focus of ministry. These are all questions to ask as you explore options.

One good place to start is in your own denomination. If they have a good program to the unreached, then sign up. They're set up to get you there. If their overseas ministries don't aim at the unreached, inquire if they would sponsor you to be part of such a new venture.

If you are not a part of a church or denomination that has a strong mission thrust, never fear! There are at least 600 North American Protestant Mission Agencies that you could hook up with. The list in Appendix 1 will get you started. Write and get on a few mailing lists.

Pieces of the Puzzle

Getting to the mission field is more than signing up with the right mission agency. There isn't a manual that will tell you step by step how to get there, but don't despair. Thousands and thousands of people just like yourself have done it and are having fruitful ministries overseas.

There are some basics you need to cover—ten of them are described here. They aren't things you can check off and say "done!" Each one is an area of growth, and you'll find yourself coming back to some of them over and over. You may find more pieces of the puzzle related to your specific need or leading. Great! Be sure to add them to the list.

Don't fall into the trap of trying to figure out the "least you can get away with." Getting there is only part of the goal: being effective for the Kingdom is your true purpose. Make sure you prepare yourself to do a good job.

Passionate, growing love for Jesus

This might seem obvious, but it is central. How do you describe yourself? How do your friends describe you? Jesus Is All? If your motivation is firmly rooted in your love for Jesus, this will sustain you when the going gets tough. And you'll have a love for doing what is right and a hatred for evil.

Passionate, growing love for people

Your love for the Lord will spill over into a love for people that won't allow you to treat them as "projects." This will empower you to cross cultural boundaries and love others radically different from yourself. Start now to develop the quality of *serving* people in the way that Jesus did by giving up everything and laying down his life for us.

Ministry experience with people of your own and different cultures.

Serving people isn't something you can start doing once you get there. If you truly love God and others it will show now.

Reaching out to internationals around you or going on a short-term mission can help you get a feel for working with people of other cultures. It's here that you begin to let go of ethnic pride and see the beauty in other people.

Appropriate skills

Have a legitimate reason to be in the host nation. Prepare yourself to serve the people in a tangible, desired manner. But don't get locked into your career plans or let your skills give you a sense of superiority.

Basic Bible knowledge

Get a firm footing. Arm yourself against the serious doubting and discouragement that will inevitably set in at weak and strenuous moments. You have to be ready to answer cultural and religious beliefs that go deep. You're introducing people to your Lord—be sure you know what he has to say.

Ready for anything

Learn to be flexible. Begin to do away with attitudes that require you to "nail everything down," have it done "right away," or have it done "my way— the right way." Allow God to put you through things that just don't seem to happen the way you expect— and trust him to make good come of it.

Perseverance

Just getting to the field will require perseverance. The requirements alone may be enough to discourage you, but the real tests are still to come. Practice now the art of following through on commitments to their completion. Remember that God has promised to help you do all the things he calls you to. Develop the quality of *permanence*.

Love for the church

Don't "escape" to the mission field. There are too many people who have gone overseas just to get away from the church or American culture. It's OK to be discerning about evils in the church and our country, but remember that our battle is against the evil, not the institutions. Develop a wholesome desire for the church's betterment and a genuine love for her people.

Study the host nation

Learn all you can about the people you are going to serve before you go. Get to know their history. Study their art forms, economics, politics and recreation. Remember that this is an ongoing process once you arrive.

Link up

Make sure you have a support group that is sending you—your fellowship or church—people who know you inside out. Allow them to be your partners in the task, not simply your bankroller. Get tied in with an agency that will effectively prepare and nurture you.

Missionaries are still needed today—lots of them. If God is putting it on your heart to be a career missionary, then give it all you have. And remember to persevere. If he has called you to something, he will be faithful to take you to its completion.

CHAPTER THIRTEEN

Counter-Cultural Servants

"I want to make Satan so nervous about my activities here in the States that he would wish I would go be a missionary!"

That's how a friend of mine described his vision of how he hoped the Lord would use him. My friend understands the church's mandate to make disciples of all nations, and he wants his life to count in that task. He is convinced that he can contribute just as much to reaching the unreached through his ministry at home as he would by being a missionary.

He has an ambition that is every bit as motivating as Paul's ambition to keep pushing back the frontiers of the gospel. He wants to stir *other Christians* to see God's heart for the world to help them take up their responsibility in the cause.

There is an urgent need for Christians like my friend, who have grasped the biblical worldview, to help wake the church up to all that is on God's heart. It is every bit as important a role as the missionary's. And it is thoroughly counter-cultural.

There's no neat job description, and precious few role models. To understand what kind of role the counter-cultural servant plays, we first need a handle on the local church and the various functions within it. I believe there are three kinds of people necessary to the proper functioning of the local church (and every member should fit primarily into one of these): the pastoral, the prophetic and the global. Let's see how they work together.

People in the *Pastoral* role nurture the saints and equip them for ministry. Pastoral gifts are essential as

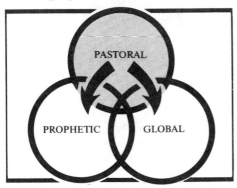

long as Christians have needs and as long as there are non-Christians in the community around them.

The Pastoral has a unique ministry to the Prophetic and Global. These two roles are so activist that they often forget that individuals have needs. You probably know people who are task-oriented rather than people-oriented. The Pastoral constantly reminds these activists that you can't overlook or abuse people while trying to accomplish spiritual ends.

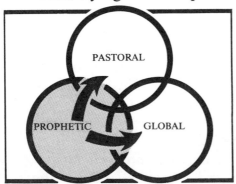

Christians who focus on the *Prophetic* role call church members to live out the counter-cultural values of the Bible. They warn the church when it starts to take on the cultural mold, and they call the Pastoral to avoid the pitfall of trying so hard to "be all things to all men" for the sake of reaching some, that it loses some of its salt.

Prophetic people are particularly sensitive to the call of the church to be involved in mercy ministries—

feeding, freeing, housing, visiting, clothing and healing the needy. They remind the Pastoral of the church's responsibility on the local and national levels and prod the Global to ensure that its ministries don't focus exclusively on spiritual needs.

People concerned for the *Global* role see the world as their parish. They understand so clearly that God's call is to all the nations that they can't rest until the church has fully engaged itself in this task. The Global seeks to nurture potential missionaries from local churches and ensures that funding for unreached peoples and other global needs is a priority in church budgets.

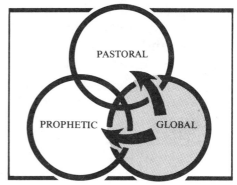

The Global speaks to the Pastoral because the world vision of the Pastoral easily fades away as nurture ministries expand. And the Global teaches the Pastoral to *love* people of other nations by challenging stereotypes and prejudices borrowed from the culture around them. The Global sensitizes the Pastoral concerning our nation's global image and suggests how the Pastoral might live to reflect global needs and resources. The Global also helps the Prophetic keep the needs of the whole world in sight while they struggle to transform lives and structures within their own culture and nation.

A Case of Imbalance

The church in the U.S. today is desperately in need of people to fulfill the Global role. It's my hunch that

God will be guiding many people in the next few years to take on this function.

Our missionary efforts to the unreached will be crippled if there isn't a strong home base of supportive people who are sold out to the cause of showing all peoples Christ's love. The need for a shaking up in our churches today is obvious. We're spending huge amounts of money on buildings, programs, even the fancy clothes we wear and the cars we drive to church on Sunday, while the average Christian gives less than $15 each year to missions.

Jonah had to be swallowed by a whale before he would even consider going to Ninevah. Our disregard for the thing closest to God's heart is as blatant a defiance of God as Jonah's disobedience.

How many times have you heard prayers in church thanking God for the freedom to worship and the abundant material "blessings" he has showered on us? Well, Jonah was thankful too. He sat in the belly of the whale rejoicing that God had saved *him*, and crowing that others could receive that grace if they'd only give up their idols. Great—Jonah had his theology right, but he still had to be *told* to go to Ninevah after the whale spat him out.

All of our prayers of thanksgiving are mocking at God's death on the cross for all the nations if our gratitude doesn't make a difference in the way we spend our time, money and talents for the nations. God deserves more than $15 a year from the richest Christians in the world.

The prophet Haggai, who played a Global role, exhorted the nation of Israel for paneling their houses while the temple lay in ruins (Haggai 1:4). His message was clear—how can we be busying ourselves with bettering our lives while the nations have no way to know or worship the true God? We need Haggais in our church today!

And our Haggais need to love the people they're speaking to. All too often the person with vision for the world gets angry at people and churches when they don't seem to hear. We need to be angry at the *sin* that keeps people from hearing.

The goal of the counter-cultural servant must be to *equip* the church to take on Christ's global passion, *not* to punish it for neglecting to do so! The heart of our Haggais have to overflow with passion to serve and build the people they speak to.

Taking Steps to Keep the Vision

The counter-cultural servant needs to take care that his vision for the nations is kept alive and growing.

Probably the greatest aid in my life is having relationships with people from other nations who are yet outside the Kingdom. I strongly encourage mission activists to get in some cross-cultural time and develop personal relationships to reinforce the vision. Culturally, we are experience-oriented people and this has affected us more than we realize. We need concrete experiences to keep our vision burning.

The people you read about in chapter one are real, and they spur me on every day.

Information

Keep the materials coming your way. Understanding what is happening around the world will push you forward. Read books, magazines, both secular and missionary, take a course in missions, receive missionary prayer bulletins. Mission agencies would love to send you their regular circulars and publications if it would help you keep the vision.

Set specific goals for yourself—so many books per month, for example—and ask God to help you keep them. There is a list of resources in Appendix 2 that will help you get started. Money spent on building your world vision is money well spent.

Linkages

Fellowship is vital. Make sure you are teamed up with people of similar heart. Coals that sit alone die out after a while. The Association of Church Missions Committees (P.O. Box ACMC, Wheaton, IL 60189) is designed to help you influence your church. Request their newsletter and be encouraged by the news you'll find in there of other churches catching the vision.

The longer you stay in your home culture, the easier it will be to slip into that culture's worldview. Expect the struggles of Big Chill country. This will be your battle ground from time to time, and you don't want to be caught off guard.

CHAPTER FOURTEEN

Gideon Was a Wimp

Gideon was a young man, probably in his 20's or 30's, when God called him to lead a band of 300 men to conquer 135,000 Midianites. It was an amazing victory.

How did it happen? What spurred Gideon on? He was the weakest and least important person in Israel.

The nation of Israel wasn't exactly reaching out to other nations at this time. Because of their sinful lives, God allowed them to be overrun by other nations. The land was completely devastated, and the Israelites were in pretty sad shape. Judges 6:1-6 describes them as fearful, hiding in caves, oppressed, discouraged and helpless.

What a mockery! This nation's God was supposedly the God of all nations and all peoples!

Enter Gideon. This young, insignificant man received a visit from an ordinary-looking angel. Gideon was sheepishly threshing a few handfuls of wheat, all the while fearing that the Midianites might come and steal even that away from him.

Listen to the angel's first words to Gideon:

"The Lord is with you, mighty warrior!" (6:12).

Gideon must have wondered if this guy had the wrong address. Wasn't it obvious that he was "none of the above?" But the angel persisted:

"Gideon, go in the strength you have and save Israel

out of Midian's hand. Am I not sending you?" (6:14).

Well, Gideon realized that the angel just didn't know who he was talking to, so he decided to set him straight about his credentials.

"But Lord, how can I save Israel? My clan is the *weakest* in Manasseh, and I am the *least* in my family" (6:15).

For some reason, Gideon thought that mattered. Everything he said about himself was true. But God chose *him*, the weakest one in Israel. After all, he could have contacted more qualified people had he wanted to! God explained it to Gideon:

"I will be with you and you will strike down the Midianites as if they were but one man" (6:16).

God used similar words many times as he called his people to make his glory known. Moses had told the Lord:

"Who am I that I should go to Pharaoh and bring the Israelites out of Egypt?" (Exodus 3:11).

The Lord simply told him: "*I will be with you*" (3:12).

And when the Lord was telling the Israelites through the prophet Haggai to move ahead with the work of the temple, his words to them were: "Be strong and work, *for I am with you*" (Haggai 2:4).

Nothing is too difficult for the Lord. *He* is the one who strengthens and equips. God isn't looking for super-heroes to do his work. He's looking for ordinary folks—you and me. He can use each one of us to reach this world with his love.

You may find yourself doubting as you look at this big world of ours. It sccms unreachable in so many ways. But God *can* use us to reach this world, and more than that, he *wants* to.

He desires to touch other people's lives through us. He is not going to touch the world with a computer or a radio. He is going to touch the world with people— individuals like you and me.

Allow God to use you to touch people that couldn't otherwise be touched, to reach nations that couldn't otherwise be reached.

Remember Jesus' last words to his followers? He commanded them to disciple all the nations. But do you remember the promise he gave with the command?

And surely I will be with you always.

Go for it! You've got all the resources of heaven backing you up!

Some Agencies You Could Join Up With Right Now

This is just a sampling of the many mission agencies. For a complete listing write to MARC, 919 W. Huntington Dr., Monrovia, CA 91016.

Interdenominational Agencies

AFRICA INLAND MISSION
P.O. Box 178
Pearl River, NY 10965
(416) 751-6077
Date organized: 1895
Home staff: 53
Field staff: 511
Length of service: A short-term program of 2-3 years and long-term service.
Skills openings: Evangelism, church planting, education, aviation, leadership.
Financial policy: Raise your own support.
Areas: Sub-Saharan Africa.
Brief description: AIM is dedicated to the work of evangelism, church planting, and church growth.

THE EVANGELICAL ALLIANCE MISSION
(TEAM)
P.O. Box 969
Wheaton, IL 60187
(312) 653-5300

Date organized: 1890
Home staff: 79
Field staff: 905
Length of service: Short-term program of one month to two years and long-term service.
Skill openings: Evangelism, church planting, development, education, literature, linguistics, medicine and radio.
Financial policy: Raise your own support.
Areas: More than twenty countries around the world.
Brief description: Of evangelical tradition, TEAM is committed primarily to evangelism, church planting and development.

GOSPEL MISSIONARY UNION
1000 North Oak
Kansas City, MO 64155
(816) 734-8500
Date organized: 1892
Home staff: 32
Field staff: 389
Length of service: A short-term program of three months to two years and long-term service.
Skill openings: Evangelism, literature production, radio and television production, development of human resources.
Financial policy: Raise your own support.
Areas: More than twenty countries in Africa, Europe and Latin America.
Brief description: Of evangelical and Baptist tradition, Gospel Missionary Union establishes churches and is engaged in evangelism through specialized services.

GREATER EUROPE MISSION
P.O. Box 668
Wheaton, IL 60187
(312) 462-8050
Date organized: 1949
Home staff: 34
Field staff: 160
Length of service: A short-term program of one to two years and long-term service.
Skill openings: Evangelism, literature distribution, theological education and theological education by extension.
Financial policy: Raise your own support.
Areas: Europe.
Brief description: Greater Europe Mission establishes churches and is engaged in evangelism through specialized services.

LATIN AMERICA MISSION
P.O. Box 341368
Coral Gables, FL 33134
(305) 444-6228
Date organized: 1921
Home staff: 22
Field staff: 164
Length of service: A short-term program of six weeks to two years and long-term sevice.
Skill openings: Evangelism, education, mass media and social services.
Financial policy: Raise your own support.
Areas: Latin America.
Brief description: Of evangelical tradition, LAM evangelizes in Latin America.

MISSION AVIATION FELLOWSHIP
P.O. Box 202
Redlands, CA 92373
(714) 794-1151
Date organized: 1944
Home staff: 65
Field staff: 240
Length of service: A short-term program of one to two years and long-term service.
Skill openings: Aviation, radio, health, and technical assistance.
Financial policy: Raise your own support.
Areas: More than twenty countries in Africa, Latin America and Southeast Asia.
Brief description: A specialized service agency of evangelical tradition supplying assistance to national churches and other agencies.

NEW TRIBES MISSION
1000 East First Street
Sanford, FL 32771
(305) 323-3430
Date organized: 1942
Home staff: Not reported.
Field staff: 1,385
Length of service: A short-term program from two months and up and long-term service.
Skill openings: Linguistics, literacy, aviation, broadcasting, Bible translation, evangelism and church planting.
Financial policy: Raise your own support.
Areas: More than twenty countries in Africa, Asia and Latin America.
Brief description: Of fundamentalist tradition, New

Tribes Mission seeks to evangelize and establish churches among unreached tribal people.

OVERSEAS MISSIONARY FELLOWSHIP
404 South Church Street
Robesonia, PA 19551
(215) 693-5881
Date organized: 1865
Home staff: 6
Field staff: 203
Length of service: A short-term program of 1-4 years and long-term service.
Skill openings: Evangelism, church planting, medicine, Bible translation, literature production and distribution.
Financial policy: Board provides support.
Areas: East Asia and France.
Brief description: An international agency of evangelical tradition establishing churches and engaged in evangelism and support of national churches.

SUDAN INTERIOR MISSION
2 Woodstone Drive
Cedar Grove, NJ 07009
(201) 857-1100
Date organized: 1893
Home staff: 128
Field staff: 590
Length of service: A short-term program of two or three months to two years and long-term service.
Skill openings: Evangelism, education, literature, medicine, linguistics, translation, literacy, broadcasting, agriculture and community development.
Financial policy: Raise your own support.

Areas: Sub-Saharan Africa.
Brief description: An international agency of evangelical tradition, SIM establishes churches and assists national churches.

WYCLIFFE BIBLE TRANSLATORS
19891 Beach Blvd.
Huntington Beach, CA 92648
(714) 536-9346
Date organized: 1935
Home staff: Information not available.
Field staff: 5,350
Length of service: Short-term programs of one week to five years and long-term service.
Skill openings: Bible translation, aviation, training, literacy and linguistics.
Financial policy: Raise your own support.
Areas: More than fifty countries around the world.
Brief description: Wycliffe is an international parent organization for 18 international sending agencies. Affiliated with Summer Institute of Linguistics (SIL), Jungle Aviation and Radio Service, and Wycliffe Associates.

Denominational Agencies
ASSEMBLIES OF GOD, DIVISION OF FOREIGN MISSION
1445 Booneville Avenue
Springfield, MI 65802
(417) 862-2781
Date organized: 1914
Home staff: 38
Field staff: 1,214
Length of service: A short-term program of one week to

two years and long-term service.

Skill openings: Evangelism, church planting, training of national leaders, theological education by extension, correspondence courses, literature publication and distribution.

Financial policy: Raise your own support.

Areas: Over 100 countries around the world.

Brief description: This agency of Pentecostal and evangelical tradition does evangelism, establishes churches and trains national church workers.

CHRISTIAN AND MISSIONARY ALLIANCE
P.O. Box C
Nyack, NY 10960
(914) 353-0750
Date organized: 1887
Home staff: 18
Field staff: 809
Length of service: A short-term program of one to two years and long-term service.
Skill openings: Literature production and distribution, theological education, Bible translation, radio and television broadcasting, evangelism and church planting.
Financial policy: Board provides support.
Areas: More than fifty countries around the world.
Brief description: CMA, an agency of evangelical tradition, establishes churches and is engaged in specialized services.

CHRISTIAN REFORMED BOARD FOR WORLD MISSIONS
2850 Kalamazoo Avenue Southeast
Grand Rapids, MI 49560

(616) 241-6568
Date organized: 1888
Home staff: 16
Field staff: 258
Length of service: A short-term program and long-term service.
Skill openings: Aviation, broadcasting, education, mass evangelism, Bible translation, medicine and church planting.
Financial policy: Board provides support.
Areas: More than twenty countries around the world.
Brief description: This agency of Reformed tradition is engaged in church planting, evangelism, and several specialized services.

CHURCH OF GOD WORLD MISSIONS
Keith at 25th Street, Northwest
Cleveland, TN 37311
(615) 472-3361
Date organized: 1886
Home staff: 9
Field staff: 78
Length of service: No short-term program but opportunity for long-term service.
Skill openings: Church planting, education, and church construction.
Financial policy: Board provides support.
Areas: More than eighty countries around the world.
Brief description: This agency of evangelical, Holiness and Pentecostal tradition is involved in church planting, church construction, and education.

CHURCH OF THE NAZARENE, GENERAL BOARD DEPARTMENT OF WORLD MISSION

P.O. Box 655
Fergus Falls, MN 56537
(218) 736-5666
Date organized: 1900
Home staff: 7
Field staff: 484
Length of service: A short-term program of two to four years and long-term service.
Skill openings: Evangelism, church planting, relief, Bible translation and distribution, education, literature and medicine.
Financial policy: Board provides support.
Areas: More than sixty countries around the world.
Brief description: Of Wesleyan tradition, the Church of the Nazarene is engaged in evangelism, church planting and support of national churches.

CONSERVATIVE BAPTIST FOREIGN MISSION SOCIETY

P.O. Box 5
Wheaton, IL 60187
(312) 665-1200
Date organized: 1943
Home staff: Not reported
Field staff: 501
Length of service: A short-term program of three months to two years and long-term service.
Skill openings: Evangelism, church planting, education, literature, linguistics, medicine and radio.
Financial policy: Raise your own support.
Areas: More than twenty countries around the world.

Brief description: The CBFMS focuses on establishing churches and serving national churches.

LUTHERAN CHURCH-MISSOURI SYNOD
500 North Broadway
St. Louis, MO 63102
(314) 231-6969
Date organized: 1847
Home staff: 11
Field staff: 254
Length of service: A short-term program of two to six years and long-term service.
Skill openings: Education, broadcasting, correspondence courses, literature, literacy, research, evangelism and church planting.
Financial policy: Board provides support.
Areas: More than thirty countries around the world.
Brief description: The LCMS establishes churches and is engaged in a variety of services.

MENNONITE CENTRAL COMMITTEE
21 South 12th Street
Akron, PA 17501
(717) 859-1151
Date organized: 1920
Home staff: 32
Field staff: 431
Length of service: No short-term program, but opportunity for long-term service.
Skill openings: Community development, secular education, agricultural assistance, relief, medicine, and self-help projects.
Financial policy: Board provides support.
Areas: More than forty countries around the world.

Brief description: A specialized sending agency of Mennonite tradition acting as a relief and service agency of the Mennonite and Brethren in Christ churches in North America.

MISSION TO THE WORLD (PRESBYTERIAN CHURCH IN AMERICA)
P.O. Box 1744
Decatur, GA 30031
(404) 292-8345
Date organized: 1973
Home staff: 19
Field staff: 134
Length of service: A short-term program of 2 years and long-term service.
Skill openings: Bible translation, evangelism, theological and general Christian education.
Financial policy: Board provides support.
Areas: More than 25 countries around the world.
Brief description: Mission to the World, of Presbyterian and Reformed tradition, establishes churches and is engaged in evangelism and education.

SOUTHERN BAPTIST CONVENTION, FOREIGN MISSION BOARD
P.O. Box 6597
Richmond, VA 23230
(804) 353-0151
Date organized: 1845
Home staff: 46
Field staff: 2,906
Length of service: A short-term of summer up to two years and long-term service.
Skill openings: Relief, development of human resour-

ces, radio and television broadcasting, medicine, evangelism and church planting.
Financial policy: Board provides support.
Areas: More than 90 countries around the world.
Brief description: The Southern Baptist Convention does evangelism and church planting as well as engaging in several specialized services.

Non-Traditional Agencies
CHRIST IS THE ANSWER
P.O. Box 12863
El Paso, TX 79913-0863
(915) 581-8179
Date organized: 1972
Home staff: 21
Field staff: 400
Length of service: 1 to 2 years
Skills openings: Mechanics, cooks, musicians, recording engineers, truck drivers, nurses, dieticians, teachers, evangelists.
Financial policy: Each team responsible for raising own support
Areas: Italy, India, Sri Lanka, Pakistan, Philippines, Portugal, Spain, Mexico, U.S., (wherever invited).
Brief description: Full-time overseas evangelism in large teams through crusades, feeding and shelter programs.

FELLOWSHIP OF ARTISTS FOR CULTURAL EVANGELISM (FACE)
1605 E. Elizabeth
Pasadena, CA 91104
(818) 794-7970
Date organized: 1977

Home staff: 5
Field staff: 3 research associates
Length of service: None.
Skills openings: Interest in ethnic arts in missions.
Financial policy: Home staff raise own support; research associates supported independently.
Area: Ethnic arts as a means of communicating the gospel.
Brief description: FACE is involved in education and mobilization of artists for cross-cultural missions, and education of missionaries in ethnic arts.

FRONTIERS
1610 E. Elizabeth
Pasadena, CA 91104
(818) 798-0807
Date organized: 1983
Home staff: 14
Field staff: 48 (170 candidates and appointees).
Length of service: 2 years minimum.
Skills openings: Experience, leadership, training in discipleship, public relations, graphics, ministry people for field.
Financial policy: Raise own support.
Areas: Muslim world.
Brief description: Exclusive focus on sending teams to do church planting in the Muslim world.

LANGUAGE INSTITUTE FOR EVANGELISM (LIFE)
P.O. Box 200
San Dimas, CA 91773
(714) 599-8491
Date organized: 1964

Home staff: 15
Field staff: 48 (plus 135 summer).
Length of service: Short-term programs from three months to three years and long-term service.
Skills openings: Good relationship skills, proven ministry experience, love and vision for Japanese people, interest in church development and church growth.
Financial policy: Raise own support.
Area: Japan.
Brief description: LIFE missionaries teach English to Japanese, working through local churches.

OPERATION MOBILIZATION
P.O. Box 148
Midland Park, NJ 07432
(201) 423-4551
Date organized: 1957
Home staff: 85-100 in offices in 25 countries.
Field staff: 1,700 plus 1,300 in summer (20 percent are from North America).
Length of service: Minimum 2-3 months.
Skills: Marine specialists for two ships; clerical/administrative; others willing to come work.
Financial policy: Raise own support—not allowed to appeal for funds.
Area: Major focus on Muslims; India is largest field (80 percent national workers).
Brief description: OM is a training movement specializing in cross-cultural evangelistic and discipleship teams around the world and on two ships.

YOUTH WITH A MISSION (YWAM)
P.O. Box YWAM
Tyler, TX 75710
(214) 597-1171
Date organized: 1960
Home staff: 70 locations all over the world—about 3,000 long- term staff around the world.
Foreign staff: About 8,000 go through short-term programs annually.
Length of service: Varies with program, most around 5 months.
Skills: Most skills used; especially creative evangelism, logistics, communications.
Financial policy: Raise own support.
Areas: Every continent, (Pacific and Asia, North and South America, Europe and Africa), sites determined by individual bases or groups of bases.
Brief description: YWAM mobilizes and trains young people for dynamic participation in world evangelization.

Resources for World Christians

Books

Bryant, David. *With Concerts of Prayer: Christians Joined for Spiritual Awakening in World Evangelization.* Ventura, CA: Regal, 1984.

Bryant, David. *How to Create World Christian Bible Studies.* Madison, WI: Inter-Varsity Missions, 1979.

Bryant, David. *In the Gap: What it Means to be a World Christian.* Ventura: Regal, 1984.

Coleman, Robert E. *The Master Plan of Evangelism.* Old Tappen, NJ: Revell, 1964.

Dayton, Edward R. and Samuel Wilson. *Unreached Peoples 79-84.* Monrovia, CA: MARC.

Donovan, Vincent J. *Christianity Rediscovered.* Maryknoll, NY: Orbis, 1978.

Elliot, Elisabeth. *The Shadow of the Almighty.* Grand Rapids, MI: Zondervan, 1958.

Goldsmith, Martin. *Don't Just Stand There.* Downers Grove, IL: InterVarsity Press, 1978.

Griffiths, Michael C. *The Church and World Mission.* Grand Rapids, MI: Zondervan, 1983.

Hopler, Thom. *A World of Difference: Following Christ Beyond Your Cultural Walls.* Downers Grove, IL: InterVarsity Press, 1978.

Howard, David M. *Student Power in World Missions.* Downers Grove, IL: InterVarsity Press, 1977.

Johnstone, Patrick J. *Operation World: A Handbook for World Intercession*. Midland Park, NJ: Send the Light, 1978.

Jones, E. Stanley. *The Unshakeable Kingdom and the Unchanging Person*. Nashville: Abingdon, 1972.

Kraybill, Don. *The Upside-Down Kingdom*. Scottsdale, PA: Herald Press, 1983.

McQuilkin, Robertson. *The Great Omission*. Grand Rapids, MI: Baker, 1984.

Olson, Bruce. *Bruchko*. Carol Stream, IL: Creation House, 1978.

Perkins, John. *With Justice for All*. Ventura, CA: Regal, 1982.

Richardson, Don. *Eternity in Their Hearts*. Ventura, CA: Regal, 1981.

Sanders, Debra, ed. *Journey to the Nations*. Pasadena, CA: Caleb Project (1605 Elizabeth St., Pasadena, CA 91104), 1983.

Sider, Ron. *Rich Christians in an Age of Hunger,* revised edition. Downers Grove, IL: InterVarsity Press, 1984.

Sine, Tom. *The Mustard Seed Conspiracy*. Waco, TX: Word, 1981.

Summer Ministry Opportunities, Student Missionary Union, Biola University, 13800 Biola Ave., La Mirada, CA 90639.

Tucker, Ruth. *From Jerusalem to Irian Jaya: A Biographical History of Christian Missions*. Grand Rapids, MI: Zondervan, 1983.

Wagner, C. Peter. *On the Crest of the Wave: Becoming a World Christian*. Ventura, CA: Regal, 1983.

Wallis, Jim. *Revive Us Again*. Nashville: Abingdon, 1983.

White, John. *The Golden Cow: Materialism in the*

Twentieth Century Church. Downers Grove, IL: Inter-Varsity Press, 1979.

Wilson, J. Christy. *Today's Tentmakers.* Wheaton, IL: Tyndale, 1979.

Winter, Ralph D. and Steven C. Hawthorne. *Perspectives on the World Christian Movement.* Pasadena: William Carey Library, 1982.

Yoder, John Howard. *The Politics of Jesus.* Grand Rapids, MI: Eerdmans, 1972.

You Can So Get There From Here. Mission Advance Research and Communication (919 W. Huntington Dr., Monrovia, CA 91016), 1981.

Periodicals

CHRISTIAN AND MISSIONS MAGAZINES:

Evangelical Mission Information Service (EMIS)
P.O. Box 794
Wheaton, IL 60187
$40/year provides: *Evangelical Missions Quarterly* and *Missionary News Service. Pulse*s (area newsletters covering Africa, Asia, Europe, Latin America, Chinese World, Muslim World) are $25/year.

Global Prayer Digest
Frontier Fellowship
P.O. Box 9
Pasadena, CA 91109
(818) 797-1111
Monthly; publishes a daily devotional focusing on the frontiers in missions through the Bible, biographies, global reports, and unreached peoples profiles. $6/year.

Global Report
P.O. Box WEF
Wheaton, IL 60189
A monthly newsletter published by the World Evangelical Fellowship, free upon request.

International Bulletin of Missionary Research
Circulation Department
P.O. Box 1308-E
Fort Lee, NJ, 07024-9958
A quarterly research bulletin dealing with scholarly issues in missions. Published by the Overseas Ministries Study Center. $12/year.

International Journal of Frontier Missions
1605 Elizabeth St.
Pasadena, CA 91104
Quarterly journal published for student leaders featuring current field and mobilization issues in frontier missions. $15/year.

The Other Side
300 W. Apsley St.
Philadelphia, PA 19144
A monthly magazine from Jubilee Ministries. Deals with radical discipleship. $16.75/year.

Sojourners
P.O. Box 29272
Washington, D.C. 20017
A monthly magazine emphasizing issues of peace-making, community and social justice. $15/year.

Together
World Vision International
919 W. Huntington Dr.
Monrovia, CA 91016
A quarterly journal of World Vision International for Christians involved in ministry to the poor in the two-thirds world. $25/year.

Urban Missions
P.O. Box 27009
Philadelphia, PA 19118
A journal focusing on urban ministry, published five times a year by Westminster Theological Seminary. $9/year.

WHEREVER Magazine
P.O. Box 969
Wheaton, IL 60189-0969
A magazine published by TEAM for young adults. Free upon request to college or seminary grads under 30. Three issues/year.

The Wittenburg Door
1224 Greenfield Dr.
El Cajon, CA 92021
The funniest and at times most insightful monthly you can receive. Aimed at reform and renewal of the church. $16.75/year.

WORLD CHRISTIAN Magazine
P.O. Box 40010
Pasadena, CA 91104
The magazine of commitment and activism for world changers. Published bi-monthly. $12/year

$18/year outside U.S.

World Evangelization Information Bulletin
P.O. Box 1100
Wheaton, IL 60189
A monthly news publication from the Lausanne Committee for World Evangelization. Available for contribution to cover expenses, if possible.

SECULAR PUBLICATIONS THAT ARE GOOD
SOURCES OF INFORMATION ON THE
WORLD:

Americas (The Inter-American Magazine)
Subscription Service Dept.
P.O. Box 973
Farmingdale, NY 11737
News and culture from Latin America.

World Press Review
P.O. Box 915
Farmingdale, NY 11737
Monthly news and views from the foreign press.

Christian Science Monitor
One Norway St.
Boston, MA 02115
Good daily international reporting.

Far Eastern Economic Review
G.P.O. Box 160
HONG KONG
Good digest of Asian news.

National Geographic
17th 7 M Street NW
Washington, D.C. 20036
Popular look at the peoples of the world.

New York Times
2229 W. 43rd St.
New York, NY 10036
Good daily international news reporting.

South, The Third World Magazine
South Publications Ltd.
Circulations Department
13th Floor, New Zealand House
80 Haymarket
London SW1Y 4TS
ENGLAND
Monthly news from a non-Western perspective.

TRAINING OPPORTUNITIES

ACMC National Conference
P.O. Box ACMC
Wheaton, IL 60187
(312) 260-1660
An association of church mission committees which
conducts a national conference in the summer. Also
have area representatives that can conduct leadership
training seminars in your church.

Biola University
13800 Biola Ave.
La Mirada, CA 90639
(213) 941-3224

Offers 3-year M.A. degree in intercultural studies.

Chinese Awareness Seminar
Chinese World Mission Center
1605 E. Elizabeth St.
Pasadena, CA 91104
(213) 684-0004
Upon invitation conducts a 1-1/2 day introductory seminar on the Chinese world for Christian audiences.

Columbia Bible College
P.O. Box 3122
Columbia, SC 29230
(803) 754-4100
Offers 3-year M.Div. or 1-year graduate certificate in Bible with a strong missions emphasis. Studies can be started by correspondence through their BEE program.

Fuller School of World Mission
Fuller Theological Seminary
135 N. Oakland Ave.
Pasadena, CA 91101
(213) 449-1745
Offers a 2-year M.A. program in cross-cultural studies for prefield missionaries. This program can be started by correspondence study. Also offers a variety of 10-day courses through its summer institutes.

Gordon-Conwell Theological Seminary
So. Hamilton, MA 01982
(617) 468-7111
Offers M.Div. degrees with an emphasis in missions.

Institute of International Studies (IIS)
1605 Elizabeth St.
Pasadena, CA 91104
(818) 797-4605
Offers a 5-week introductory college study program on world evangelization called "PERSPECTIVES." Conducts one-week teacher training workshops in winter and summer to train their alumni to conduct its program in their own area.

Missionary Internship (MI)
P.O. Box 457
Farmington, MI 48024
(313) 474-9110
Offers training programs for new and furloughing missionaries.

Muslim Awareness Seminar
Samuel Zwemer Institute
P.O. Box 365
Altadena, CA 91001
(818) 794-1121
Upon invitation conducts a 1-1/2 day introductory seminar on the Muslim Ministry for Christian audiences.

Overseas Ministries Study Center (OMSC)
6315 Ocean Dr.
Ventnor, NJ 08406
(609) 823-6671
Offers issue-oriented workshops for missionaries, students, and church leaders led by mission leaders from around the world.

School of World Mission and Evangelism
Trinity Evangelical Divinity School
2045 Half Day Rd.
Bannockburn, Deerfield, IL 60015
(312) 945-8800
Offers 3-year M.Div. degrees with an emphasis in missions.

URBANA
Inter-Varsity Missions
233 Langdon St.
Madison, WI 53703
(608) 257-1103
Offers tri-annual missionary conventions at Urbana, Illinois, geared to college-age students.

Wheaton College
Wheaton, IL 60187
(312) 260-5195
Offers M.A. programs with emphasis in missions. Also conducts short mission courses through the Billy Graham Center in the summer.

William Carey International University
1539 E. Howard St.
Pasadena, CA 91104
(818) 797-1200
Offers M.A. and Ph.D. degrees in TESOL, Community Development, and Cultural Studies.

CURRICULUM

Change the World School of Prayer
Change the World Ministries

P.O. Box 5838
Mission Hills, CA 91345
(213) 782-1216
A one-day video seminar on intercessory prayer featuring Dick Eastman.

Hearing and Doing
Partnership in Mission, Inc.
1564 Edge Hill Rd.
Abington, PA 19001
A learning package on gospel and culture for small groups. Includes audio tapes, worksheets, and leader's guide.

An Introduction to Christian Community Development
G L Media
2300 Knoll Drive
Ventura, CA 93003
1 (800) 235-3411 outside CA
1 (800) 342-3631 inside CA
This video series presents three of the most powerful messages by John Perkins. 45 minutes each.

Language Learning and Mission: A Video Seminar
Lingua House
135 N. Oakland Ave.
Pasadena, CA 91101-1790
(818) 449-1745, ext. 3711
An 18-hour video training curriculum for orientating summer and short-term missionaries on language and culture learning. Features Dr. Tom Brewster.

The Local Church Can Change the World
ACMC
P.O. Box ACMC
Wheaton, IL 60189
(312) 260-1660
Offers a 5-hour planning seminar with slides for mission committee leadership.

The Luna Game
WORLD CHRISTIAN Magazine
P.O. Box 40010
Pasadena, CA 91104
(818) 797-5320
A 50-minute cross-cultural communication experience for groups from 15 on up.

Strategies for Living Seminar
World Vision International
919 W. Huntington Dr.
Monrovia, CA 91016
(818) 357-7979
A managing-your-time seminar available by video tapes and workbooks.

World Christian Video Training Curriculum
Inter-Varsity Missions
233 Langdon St.
Madison, WI 53703
(608) 257-0263
Consists of 3 video seminars by David Bryant combining the best of media design with teaching on the world mission of the church.